Dearest

Eluna Mara

Truly Inspirational ♡

love

Liz ♡

Become
Smartyr
not a
Martyr

How to hypnotize yourself in
20 minutes to
change your mind and
fulfil your dreams

Deborah Kerr & Riz Virdee

BALBOA.PRESS
A DIVISION OF HAY HOUSE

Balboa Press books may be ordered through booksellers or by contacting:

Balboa Press
A Division of Hay House
1663 Liberty Drive
Bloomington, IN 47403
www.balboapress.co.uk
UK TFN: 0800 0148647 (Toll Free inside the UK)
UK Local: 02036 956325 (+44 20 3695 6325 from outside the UK)

Print information available on the last page.

ISBN: 978-1-9822-8342-1 (sc)
ISBN: 978-1-9822-8343-8 (hc)
ISBN: 978-1-9822-8344-5 (e)

Balboa Press rev. date: 04/30/2021

Disclaimer

We chose the title Become Smartyr not a Martyr as a play on words. There is no inference on our part that you are stupid or unintelligent if you are not already a smartyr or have a smartyr mindset.

This book is not intended to replace any professional medical advice or provide personal psychological analysis. The techniques and self-hypnosis suggested in this book are not a form of clinical treatment for medical or psychological problems.

If you have any psychological or medical condition that you think might be exacerbated by the read-aloud smartyr self-hypnosis provided in this book, cease practice immediately.

However, it is rare to experience problematic effects from hypnosis, but we do advise that if you experience sudden anxiety or are struggling with anxiety before you begin, you should postpone self-hypnotic practice and seek medical advice.

Using the information in this book, we and the publishers assume no responsibility for the outcome of your decisions.

Dedications

Deborah for Matthew

✻

Rizwana for Dilara and Shaan

✻

You are our best creations

Contents

Become Smartyr not a Martyr

"Without mercy, the voice inside my head tells me, 'nobody cares, and if I am to feel loved and valued, I must do whatever it is they want me to do. Then, I can tell myself, I am good, and I will be liked, and I will feel valued.'

However, the berating persists, living rent-free in my mind telling me, 'however much I do, I'm not doing enough or making a big enough difference, and no-one values how much I am doing'.

Finally, left feeling unappreciated, I'm now overwhelmed, resentful, bitter, and confused, I'm enraged. I scream inside myself, 'it's not fair! what about me! I hate you! Am I not worth something!?'

But this suffering is short-lived because feeling ashamed, and guilty for wanting something for myself, makes me appease and atone for feeling this way.

Once again, the internal distortions start all over. A new drama and voice inside, reminds me, again and again, 'I'm the only one who can make things better!' Worthy intentions spoiled, by its adversarial tone, spinning like a non-stop tumble dryer ruining everything and reinforcing the evidence that, 'no one cares, I'm rubbish, I'm not good enough, and there must be something wrong with me'."

Foreword

It is always a thrill for an educator to see how one's students take what they were taught and make it uniquely their own. A greater thrill still is when one's former students put pen to paper and write a book. So, I can say what an absolute pleasure it was for me when graduates from one of the last courses I was to teach came to me to tell me about their project to write this book.

Deborah Kerr and Rizwana Virdee are well-skilled and accredited practitioners who were already blending EMDR into their therapeutic model when they undertook the Certificate in Hypnosis for Counsellors and Psychotherapists. The National College of Hypnosis and Psychotherapy, one of the oldest schools of hypnosis and psychotherapy in the UK, founded in 1977, added to their desire to make their model even more effective and progressive by integrating hypnosis into their already vast therapeutic portfolios.

Becoming Smartyr not a Martyr, is the culmination of their studies and work within hypnosis. While many books cover the utilization of self-hypnosis for practitioners and how they can use it to aid in their client's health and well-being, Deborah and Riz have made the idea of using self-hypnosis something that is far more user friendly for the public and gives a valuable resource for helping to take individual responsibility for one's own mental health. Of course, no book is a substitute for working with a qualified professional, and this book can be used as a resource for clients currently in therapy as well as for those who are simply in need of a mental "tune-up."

Many believe counseling or psychotherapy is utilized because something is wrong with the person presenting is a misconception that is brilliantly challenged in this book. To paraphrase Milton Erickson, the American Psychotherapy and the father of modern clinical hypnosis, clients have all the resources they need to be happy, healthy, and well. This book is a manifestation of this idea. Clients are not intrinsically broken, even those in severe mental distress. It is far more the case that clients search for a way for them to get back into some kind of rapport with their own unconscious mind. Once this is done, the psychological discourse is reduced, and real positive self-change can begin.

Through the pages of this book and exercises included, the reader is given the opportunity to become aware of their own capacity to be the hero of their life and choose not to have to be in the role of a victim. Often the first step to become smartyr not a martyr is to recognize that one has the potential to change the way they perceive themselves. Hypnosis is an excellent tool to begin to understand the metaphoric value of both the smartyr and the martyr, and to learn that it is not a binary choice to be one or the other. Rather, all of us have the capacity to have components of each of these roles within us. The "trick" is to find a balance between these components to be a fully actualized, autonomous human being.

This book gives the reader the much-needed direction for them to take the control of their own narrative and begin to reassess their life and life purpose. This book is a much-needed volume in the self-help library in that I believe that it not only discusses the benefits of taking charge of one's own mental state, but it also gives exercises and tools to make that a reality. I recommend this work for not only members of the public but also for practitioners who are looking for novel and innovative ways to employ hypnosis as part of their clinical practice. I commend this book without reservation.

Shaun J.F. Brookhouse, MA
Honorary Fellow, United Kingdom
Council for Psychotherapy
Former Principal, National College of
Hypnosis and Psychotherapy
Director, Brookhouse Hypnotherapy Ltd
President, European Association for Hypno-Psychotherapy
International Member, American
Society of Clinical Hypnosis

Introduction

We have found in our clinical practice that the victim mentality is genuinely a problem. Most people enter counseling describing themselves in a 'stuck' place, unknowingly having fallen into the realms of a victim mindset. Whether it is by being in difficult and tumultuous relationships or with a barrage of constant negative self-judgments, people unconsciously create complex layers of addictive patterns of behaviors. These include self-neglect, substance abuse, overeating, irresponsible spending, loving too much, caring too much, and even shaming and humiliating others and themselves.

Ultimately to survive, you can unconsciously fool yourself into believing that you are 'dealing with it'. As people our primary strategy is survival. Our default is to run away from feeling the emotional pain. Instead, if left untreated, you create dysfunctional protective layers of behaviors and delude yourself into believing you feel better. The addictive nature of rationalization, intellectualization, along with denial, places a dent in your personal values that reinforces negative messages in your mind. This, in turn, further embeds limiting beliefs about you, your relationships, and your reality.

Just as importantly, this book is not targeted at anyone who has suffered a real-life event, which has left them a genuine victim of circumstance. Any of us can fall victim to a real-life event or become a victim of circumstance. Being caught up in a predicament where we had no control over what happened. Nothing we did or failed to make things happen the way they did, is profoundly affecting and disturbing that can eventually be experienced as traumatic.

Being a survivor means to take action by moving through the ordeal, the pain, the grief, and loss in a holistic approach encompassing the mind and body. If not, you can find yourself unknowingly moving into victimhood and further becoming accustomed to staying in denial, trapped, and engaging in self-destructive coping behavior.

Suppose you do not heal through a mind-heart coherence and embrace the unification of wisdom-of-mind and heart-of-compassion. In that case, your victim mentality becomes programed and embedded as your personality. It will eventually establish an identity where you can no longer recognize its origins. You can end up beating yourself up and ruining valuable relationships. You become a complainer and blamer and can forget ever having made a choice to live this way.

All these reactive behaviors ultimately fight against what you truly need and want. This book is about getting you to realize that your mind and body are powerful. It is the manifestation of all thought, perception, determination, memory, emotion, and imagination that takes place within you. You can learn to adapt your consciousness to the different situations you face. You can create your smartyr Self by doing the exercises and engaging and practicing the read-aloud smartyr self-hypnosis.

As humans, we are all subject to negative thinking to some degree. This book raises your awareness and explores the defended yet typical victim's personal values and belief system, which we term here as the martyr.

We believe the first step to satisfy curiosity in all aspects of mental health is psychoeducation. As therapists, we know that providing psychoeducation and having the ability to understand another's emotional state allows our clients to share their daily struggles. This empathic attunement will enable us to help them recognize, understand, and engage how their thoughts, feelings, and behaviors are deeply rooted in their past experiences and embedded in their minds and bodies.

We have examined the relevance of the qualities of both wisdom and compassion and the need for their inter-dependence. We had to cultivate and realize our own personal values. We had to understand and reframe our subconscious and unconscious beliefs before supporting you in revealing your potential to become a better version of yourself. Therefore, we had to become the book before we could write it.

After countless hours of clinical discussions and continual professional development, we decided to demystify victimhood or martyr complexities. Collectively, having drawn upon a vast amount of personal and professional experience and having deeply related to ourselves and our clients over the years, we became ardent about making emotional health the focus. Using our professional training and personal therapy to guide us, we decided the world needed this kind of book.

We have discovered that most of our clients live their lives from victimhood which we have termed martyrdom. Most clients often enter treatment feeling lonely, bitter, depressed, and with their relationships in turmoil, either with themselves and with others, and usually not know why.

A common and recurring theme we found with our clients was that they tend to come into counseling believing that something is wrong with them or because they do not feel 'good enough'. Whether they speak about depression, anxiety, or relationship issues, they predominantly have an internalized value system where they feel they have no right to express personal needs or feelings.

Clients would also present with vague or unclear symptoms along with chronic physical conditions and feelings of shame about who they are. They would feel defective and blocked, unable to find ways to move forward. These symptoms proved to be related to them feeling stuck and caught in a loop of self-defeat.

These types of clients often have difficulty accepting unchangeable limitations in their abilities, and they struggle to believe they add value to their lives and others. Martyrs, or people living in victimhood, often feel no-one is there to support them. With an underdeveloped and inconsistent personal value system, alongside negative limiting beliefs, it is no wonder they feel misunderstood, cheated out of love, invisible or empty.

Through this frustration, we decided to create a guide to cultivate and support intrinsic self-directed growth. We aim to underpin well thought out theories to help you understand the true nature of mental and emotional concerns and deliver complex material in a simple to understand format. We have clinical experience in psychology, psychotherapy, and hypnosis for psychotherapy. It is a unique integration that brings all these aspects together to be used as a powerful tool to help fast-track your progress to become smartyr.

We are hopeful about the future of the person who reads this book. You are not just reading a book. You are cultivating a new way of life.

Is This Book for You?

Life is not just one page
It is the entire book

Chapter 1

Questionnaire

The following table provides some typical characteristics of the martyr. How many of the following statements apply to you currently? Answer the questions below, and if you answer 'yes' to ten or more of the following statements, this book is for you.

1	I haven't had anyone in my life who really understands me or can be bothered to meet my true wants, needs, and feelings	
2	People get really upset when I try to express how I feel	
3	I feel that people really take advantage of me, have wronged me, and have tried to harm me for their own purposes	
4	For most of my life, I have been mistreated by people important to me	
5	I feel isolated and alone and feel like I don't fit in, as I am different from other people	
6	It's really sad knowing that nobody would notice if I disappeared tomorrow	
7	Other people always seem to achieve so much more than me	
8	People always find something about me to criticize	
9	Other people always humiliate me by pointing out my failures and inadequacies	
10	I see that everyone else is better off than me in some way	
11	I have a hard time forgiving others when things go wrong	
12	The idea of having an anxiety attack plays heavily on my mind	
13	I'm too scared to take risks in life and therefore achieve nothing of any significance	
14	I catastrophize, and my thoughts are in a constant loop	
15	I believe my body size, gender, sexual orientation, or education is a major reason why I feel stuck and is stopping me from moving forward	
16	I never know what I want for myself; I always let others make choices for me, and I hate that	
17	I find it really hard to ask anyone to take care of my needs	

18	I often try to express the anger and resentment built up inside of me, but I find it hard	
19	I am under constant pressure to achieve and get things done	
20	What I have to offer is of great value, but no one seems to notice or appreciates me	
21	I struggle reaching my goals because I can't sacrifice my immediate gratification	
22	I make most of my life's decisions based on other people's approval	
23	It really annoys me when people blame others for their problems and make excuses for themselves	
24	Even after someone has said sorry, I still hold a grudge	
25	Because no one really cares about me, I'm always looking for other's ulterior motives	

If you think the above statements do not apply to you, then this book may not be for you. However, read on because you probably know someone who this book does apply to.

Chapter 2

What This Book is About

Life is not just one page - it is the entire book

We recognize that most people struggle to understand the stages of internal change and the mechanisms needed to create that change. Therefore, we encourage exploration and self-directed healing to raise awareness of the subconscious and unconscious programming that drives everything.

In our clinical practice, we encourage our clients to slow down and engage their bodies and minds. Over time, our clients begin to consider how their unconscious historical memories are relevant and connected to their ongoing struggles and repeating patterns that continue to manifest in their daily lives. We want to encourage you to do the same as you read this book, so you too can create change in your present moment.

We want you to become curious to engage in all aspects of self-help and personal development. We want to offer you the ability to help yourself out of some of your emotional turmoil. We want you to use this book as a retrieval process to explore undigested thoughts, patterns, and behaviors. Or as a precursor to entering the realms of therapy and making that first brave step towards meeting a therapist in real-time for co-created personal discovery.

Our fundamental approach is grounded in evidence-based therapies of transactional analysis (TA), exploring relational dynamics; rational, emotional, behavioral therapy (REBT); and cognitive-behavioral therapy (CBT), both engage your thinking; and dialectical behavioral therapy (DBT), which gets you to perform action-orientated tasks. And, hypnosis for psychotherapy, which literally reprograms your mind and overwrites your martyr mindset.

Our hypnosis training for psychotherapy has given us the ability to provide you with a series of six bespoke read-aloud smartyr self-hypnosis scripts to help you achieve incredible results. The scripts are designed to put you into a hypnotic state while you are reading aloud, as the sound of your own voice has a sedative effect on your mind and body. So, at various sections in this book, you will need to slow down and take time to digest what you read and to reflect on what you learn.

Our series of six read-aloud smartyr self-hypnosis scripts will literally hypnotize you while you read. Every time you pick up and the smartyr self-hypnosis scripts out loud, you will experience a deeper and more suggestible state of mind, enabling you to absorb the positive messages. We provide the theories and exercises to educate you to evict self-doubt, self-defeating characteristics, and negative thinking. The self-hypnosis trains your mind to reprogram negative attributes and embeds the positive messages into your subconscious through autosuggestion.

The information we provide in this book will give you the guidance you need to support you on your road to recovery and healing as you move from a reactive state to a more responsive way of being. As a survivor, you can ultimately find your own meaning from adversity, leading to wisdom, compassion, choice, and opportunity.

Creation

We aim to create personal transformation which will bring into existence a new personal reality, reconciling and differentiating between positive and negative self-generated beliefs and what you have been told about yourself from childhood, creating a smartyr identity.

Smartyrdom is about breaking the habits of martyrdom and re-evaluating your personal value system. It is an active approach that uses creativity to make a change. It is about remembering that you are worthier than you consciously believe you are.

You will need to make a practice out of self-hypnosis, as smartyrdom is fundamentally about reprogramming your mind. It is about challenging your dysfunctional beliefs and redirecting your focus on achieving self-mastery by accessing your subconscious through self-hypnotic autosuggestion.

By employing a step-by-step process and reading the self-hypnosis scripts, you will identify, evaluate, and change your negative thoughts over time. Through repetition and practice, positive and improved rational thought processes will develop more naturally.

Change

This book is about a transition towards change. You will become rich in personal power. This book will teach you to prioritize your personal values, challenge your limiting beliefs, and identify what is important to you.

When you live by your personal values, you motivate yourself to cultivate characteristics and behaviors that guide your choices in your day-to-day life and your future visions and goals – making you feel more fulfilled.

This book offers a more straightforward or less challenging path to change. It will help you unravel and understand the fundamental thoughts and beliefs that you can work through.

Encouragement

This book is about encouragement. We have worked with countless clients who operate from a position of victimhood. We realize you must find the right tools to help your victim-self process what has happened to you and learn new ways to respond.

Our book is an invitation to empathically challenge your victim mindset because there is a real victim in each of us who requires our wisdom, empathy, compassion, and humility.

Giving yourself time and space allows you to notice any negative self-talk or self-imagery you use that no longer works for you. In other words, you will learn what you say to yourself or how you see yourself when no one else is watching or listening.

It is essential to know that moving away from familiar surroundings may not be easy. Unlearning what you already know will require cognitive effort on your part. We hope to encourage you to evolve and be empowered to get the life you want and deserve.

Self-acceptance

This book is about self-acceptance. We want you to know that wisdom, compassion, and empathy are at the root of smartyrdom. We do not intend our theoretical descriptions to be an attack on victims or statements that a person is deliberately or consciously behaving in ways that cause their own pain or suffering.

Smartyrdom is not about blaming the victim. We simply want you to become familiar with the traits of martyrdom within you so that you do not continue to sabotage your own life and keep suffering. First, you must want to stop fostering the elements that create a victim mentality. The paradox is, there is no way out other than to go in. We have simply used the natural creative energy that we all possess to develop our smartyr mind.

Our intention is you become fit for the business to live a life of quality. While knowledge and understanding and the embodiment of self-compassion are fundamental for healing to happen, it also comes when you give yourself time and space to listen quietly and allow yourself to be heard deeply.

Self-Compassion

This book is a dedication to encompassing the components of wisdom and compassion. Wisdom is the intelligence of knowing how to live, and compassion nurtures the capacity to heal. Wisdom allows you to see clearly what is happening, and empathy helps heal past hurts and current life struggles. The union of these two components is inter-dependent. If you are to become a smartyr and be on the trajectory towards feeling better and cultivating a smartyr way of living, you will need to balance both wisdom and compassion.

Personal development leads to wisdom, but too much of it can lead to over-analysis, rationalization, and intellectualization and will keep you stuck. On the other hand, too much compassion leads to self-pity and martyrdom and will keep you stuck.

The road to recovery and healing means you moving from a reactive state to a more responsive way of being. As a survivor, you can ultimately find your own meaning from adversity, leading to wisdom, compassion, choice, and opportunity.

Chapter 3

What you will get

How would you like to discover new capacities, experience fulfilling relationships, and live a soul-satisfying harmonious life? You will learn how to achieve this. The read-aloud smartyr self-hypnosis scripts will allow you to absorb what you have read and embed everything you have learned.

Imagine how it feels to express your own best personal achievements and the very natural essence of who you really are. Are you ready and open? Because you can change your life. Imagine what it looks like having replaced your negative attributes with self-confidence, optimism, courage, and resilience.

Get ready for an exciting experience because this book will give you whatever you want from your life when you change your mindset. Envisage relationships without self-doubt and self-defeating behaviors and live a quality of life that you have never experienced before. That would be amazing, and it is possible!

We have the privilege to work with motivated clients who are committed and willing to invest their time in personal discovery. They come to realize their values and are dedicated to working at reprogramming the limiting beliefs that had kept them emotionally stuck for many years. When they learned to live by their new discoveries, they felt better about themselves. They became more focused on doing the things that now brings quality in their life. Our intent is to enhance your wellbeing in your mission to also becoming smartyr.

Psychoeducation

Psychoeducation is about becoming educated around psychological concepts, with the benefit of lowering the stigma around mental health that also teaches you how to help yourself.

When you actively engage in psychoeducation, it becomes a fundamental part of the therapeutic process to emphasize recovery, healing, and making a change in your life. You will need to be open to learning new information, be curious to ask questions, and participate in practicing new skills.

Our emphasis in this book is to psychoeducate you to become smartyr, not a martyr, through learning and taking action. You will learn the concepts of psychological and developmental theory. Using the principles outlined in this book, your negative thoughts will reveal themselves for you to evaluate and re-construct. Over time, through repetition and practice of the smartyr self-hypnosis scripts, positive and rational thoughts will naturally happen.

When you begin the journey towards smartyrdom, your subconscious will trigger your intentions and motivation to make the mind-heart connection, and you will naturally launch into action.

You will get a checklist that helps you identify if you fall into the realms of martyrdom. You will get a Victim to Survivor to Thriver table by Barbara Whitfield to help you track your progress. We educate you in the Drama Triangle with a comprehensive breakdown that allows you to recognize your life position.

Progressing through this book, you will expand your social skills, learn how to influence, and manage other emotions and gain a deepening awareness of empathy and compassion. You will also learn to stop thinking negatively through cognitive restructuring.

Understanding the Mind

Freud divided human consciousness into three distinct levels: the conscious, the subconscious, and the unconscious. In discussion, the subconscious mind and unconscious mind are terms that are used interchangeably. All three aspects are separate functions of one mind.

The conscious mind is our awareness in the present moment and represents all our current reality. The conscious mind thinks linearly and utilizes the left side of the brain. Its job is to maintain everything that you are familiar and regular.

The subconscious and unconscious mind utilize the right side of the brain. It does an infinite number of things independently from the conscious mind. It has access to all our memories that we have built from birth, and it stores all our values and beliefs, and it expresses all creativity.

The subconscious mind is the part of the mind that can be accessible to awareness. It is the part of the mind that is designed for change and learning. In contrast, the unconscious mind represents everything else that is entirely out of awareness.

Everything that we do that is conscious to us is a projection of both the subconscious and unconscious mind. What this means is that we do everything unconsciously first.

Therefore, did you know that your unconscious mind is in charge of you and your body without conscious deliberation? Your mind is the very epicenter of your intelligence and ultimate power but your unconscious rules the show. It drives all your thoughts and actions, both positive and negative. Your mind and body do not dispute, rationalize or analyze your thoughts, feelings, or beliefs, which have been encoded into your unconscious.

Like a computer hard drive, your mind and body have a vast capacity to permanently store and retrieve information based on everything that has ever happened to you. The data is imported and is absorbed as is - uncensored. All your encoded memories and experiences are designed to ensure that your responses obey and remain consistent with your self-image and who you believe to be. Therefore, your unconscious mind drives everything that happens to you in your life.

Fortunately, your brain is also flexible. It is possible that you can learn to reprogram your mind and reframe your negative thinking. Once you access your subconscious and become aware of your mind-heart connection, you will identify and separate your feelings from others. We want to state that discovering the distinction between yourself and others is crucial to understanding who you are and becoming a smartyr.

How to use your mind to become smartyr

Your mind is the key to your success, and you have the power to learn how to change it. In specific parts of the book, you will be invited to consider points for action.

You use your mind by making a decision.

When you decide to implement these actions, you will gain a clearer idea of what you want and begin to focus on your goals. Gaining this clarity allows your vision to be more powerful, allowing your mind to turn that vision into reality. You will begin to embody new and different experiences and break old habits of thinking and being.

You use your mind by making a commitment.

Once you become aware of how you visualize being a smartyr, you will be motivated by deliberate discipline to commit to your idea and allow that commitment to drive you. You become more prepared to push yourself to the next level, committing to overcoming any negativity and committing to a better life.

You use your mind by engaging with the series of read-aloud smartyr self-hypnosis.

Through cognitive restructuring, your mind will learn to stop thinking negatively and change subconsciously destructive stored data by flooding it and overwriting it with smartyr programming while reading aloud to yourself. When inflow, it is at this point the subconscious mind becomes activated, creating new ideas and concepts that will put you into a hypnotic state.

This is how we fast-track your subconscious mind, for you to ultimately develop your smartyr Self. You will succeed in this by using your mind to conceptually understand your hard-wiring and intentionality to actively reprogram thoughts, feelings, and patterns of behavior held in your unconscious.

When you are ready to become smartyr you will:

* engage in the principles of how your unconscious directs and influences the decisions and choices you make
* recognize which life-position you operate from
* use the powers of our six read-aloud smartyr self-hypnosis to reprogram your mind while you read and to activate your smartyr mind
* create a healthy mental diet of regular read-aloud smartyr self-hypnosis
* master the formula to develop your authentic and charismatic Self
* magnify a positive mindset and develop a smartyr identity using the smartyr self-hypnosis series that literally changes your mind as you read this book.

The smartyr self-hypnosis will help you to:

* expand your social skills and become socially adept
* influence and manage other people's emotions
* gain a deepening awareness of empathy and compassion
* stop thinking negatively through cognitive restructuring
* embody new and different experiences
* break old habits of negative thinking and unhelpful addictive behavior
* raise self-awareness, develop self-regulation and motivation
* change towards the journey of growth, maturation, and self-realization
* adapt to harmony, moments of joy, and contentment.

We suggest you engage proactively with the exercises and the series of our six read-aloud smartyr self-hypnosis. You will become conscious of the blocks you put in your way and know the beliefs you have created about yourself, for yourself and others.

We know by experience how powerful these exercises can be. Once you have garnered some insight and awareness into your mindset, the smartyr self-hypnosis will negate old patterns of negative beliefs and help towards a smartyr and growth-oriented mindset.

By the end of this book, you are going to:

* recognize a real sense of yourself, no matter how much life and people may want to sabotage it
* be acquainted with your true capabilities and successes
* find an inward satisfaction as you create the life you want
* experience your own success and a glorious vision of your future
* accomplish a zest for life and goodwill towards society who in turn help you get what you want
* feel the joy of being a smartyr, and that is the most constructive thing you can do for yourself and others.

The Martyr

A martyr creates a storm and then complains it is raining

Chapter 4

The Martyr

A martyr creates a storm and then complains it is raining

As a martyr, you suffer terribly. You are tormented by the negative self-image based on your unconscious automatic negative thoughts, rumination, and predicting catastrophic outcomes in your life. Your negative thoughts can feel reasonable and believable to you. Your intrusive thoughts, or 'thought traps' are the phrases you often use to describe your suffering.

As a martyr, you believe you have been afflicted by people and life events and feel justified in saying:

* Why does this always have to happen to me?
* If it's not one thing, it's another
* It's not my fault
* I couldn't help it
* No-one is giving as much as me
* I can't do this on my own
* I am the hardest worker
* I am unlovable.

For example, in this scenario, let us imagine you are J. D. In your family, achieving university status is not a priority as education is not in your family's value system. Therefore, you have to compromise yourself and your personal values for accomplishment and desire to design your own career. Your family's expectation is that everyone is expected to go to work, come home, have dinner, watch TV, and go to bed. Conversations are limited, and sharing feelings, having visions, and goals do not feature. This limiting space is the environment you live in. It does not occur to you to challenge your family value system and the limited beliefs you all live by. You become the effect of your family environment. As a result of this effect, from a very young age, you adopted a limiting unconscious belief that somehow you are not good enough. The unspoken message you carry from your family value system is 'don't be yourself, be who we want you to be, then you will be loved and accepted'.

As J.D., if you are seen reading a book or researching on the computer, you are ridiculed. Any attempt to grow your edges or to make a choice for yourself is thwarted. Your family system's culture is so embedded that you find yourself back in alignment with the family's expectations. Feeling disillusioned, powerless to express your true feelings, you revert to your former state of feeling only worthy when staying loyal and serving the needs of your family. Yet again, you regress, feeling worthless as your needs are unmet and aspirations denied. Change and personal growth again are compromised.

These feelings have a ripple effect in all areas of your life. As J.D., you unconsciously surround yourself with people who have similar value systems to your family as that is what is safe and familiar to you. You become confused when your partner, friends, and colleagues do not care to encourage your growth or are too self-absorbed to see, hear or understand what you want or need. It reinforces your belief that no-one really cares. You unconsciously carry self-pitying limiting beliefs about your potential in all areas of your life. Therefore, how you do one thing is how you do everything. As J.D., for you to succeed in growing your edges, you will need to feel a burning fire in your belly. You need to connect to your desire and take a leap of faith and choose to follow your desire despite the odds seemingly against you, along with the fear of the uncertainty you may face. You must choose growth and realize your own personal value system as separate from your family and friends. You must choose to become the cause of your life and not the effect of it any longer.

As J.D., you are a victim of your history. You feel agonized, burdened, distressed, oppressed, plagued, troubled, wounded, and persecuted in some shape or form to some degree. As J.D., you would have suppressed and repressed many feelings and memories. When you suppress your feelings and memories, you are subconsciously aware they are painful, and you purposefully hide them away. When you repress your feelings and memories, you have unconsciously, without knowing, hidden them.

Either way, suppression, and repression shape your personality, constellate status, and life position, impact your body and physical health, and overall quality of your life. The center of being a martyr is the unconscious pathological need to be showered with attention and depended upon by others, whether by praise or by pity which, understandably, a martyr or a victim will justify.

Martyrs express themselves on a continuum from the passive victim to the raging victim. They are multi-dimensional, not always presenting themselves as the typical 'poor me' person. Both passive and raging victims, martyrs, crave confrontation and thrive on overt or covert drama. The demeanor of the passive victim is to exhibit having no needs, wants, or desires. Whereas the raging victim's demeanor is to express their sense of entitlement and grandiosity at having needs, wants, and desires met. Again, both passive and raging victims are righteous, self-sacrificing, and have a need to feel special, something which the martyr will justifiably defend against when challenged by others. Ultimately, whether passive or raging, they are still expressing 'poor me'.

Unconsciously, the raging martyr elicits help and support from others despite the considerable stress they place upon themselves and those around them because they have trouble accepting that they have had any part to play in their problem or life situation. In contrast, the passive martyr avoids making any real bonds or forming intimate attachments out of fear of the loss associated with having a sense of worthlessness.

Wherever you are on the continuum as a passive or raging martyr, the reality is, you live in the past and have a propensity to seek revenge as you hang on to old grievances. You fear the challenge of being held accountable for something, and you will bring up old memories and events to underpin and defend your childhood hurts and emotional injuries.

In retaliation, your modus operandi, whether passive or raging, metaphorically uses weapons such as sharp swords, blunt instruments, or thin needles as legitimate reasons for your hurts as to why you cannot make changes to your attitude. Ultimately, you need to be appreciated for who you are and not what others believe you are.

Here are some characteristics that define the passive or raging martyr:

* You believe you are powerless and at the merciless helm of everyone and everything around you
* You truly believe you are out of control at being able to manage your life. You are unable to express what you need, what you desire or what you deserve in a healthy way
* You point the finger and blame your perpetuating problem as the fault of others or your environment
* You can give long lists of seemingly reasonable and justifiable explanations why you are stuck yet are unable to consider ways in which you can plan to resolve your situation
* You outwardly show you are powerful. Your perceived power is a thin veil to your manipulative skills, coercion, and calculated plans to get what you need
* You get into arguments easily and believe you are under attack all the time
* You wonder why everyone gets angry and impatient with you
* You have great difficulty in trusting people and are quite suspicious and look out for other people's ulterior motives
* You are hyper-vigilant and sensitive to abandonment and betrayal and being taken advantage of
* You feel you must protect yourself from perceived intentional hurt
* You believe others have an ulterior motive when they show love to you
* You become angry and resentful when no-one sees how much you give
* You become angry when you think about the way you have been mistreated.

Chapter 5

The Benefits of Being a Martyr

The identity of being a martyr is the mentality of viewing your life as negative and being out of control. However, many rewards keep you emotionally invested as a martyr for staying with a problematic mindset and harmful behavior patterns. It is hard to imagine how you can possibly benefit from this negative, angry, or passive manner, often masked in sadness. But believe it or not, there is a lot of benefit in you playing the martyr. You think you are gaining attention, finding value, and experiencing personal power.

As a martyr, you do not need to have an interesting life per se, as chaos and drama keep you busy and provides you with a sense of being alive. Rarely do you experience boredom, as there is little or no time to do much else. Fundamentally, any sense of boredom or feeling under-valued becomes the trigger to create chaos and draw others into a drama. A chaotic farce becomes an outlet for you to blame and complain, reinforcing the unconscious belief you are powerless to choose differently.

However, on the opposite end of the continuum, chaos and drama are not evident to the martyr who has withdrawn from life, not making close bonds, or forming deep, meaningful attachments. Instead, chaos and drama with these types of martyrs who seemingly have little going on in their lives are played out in their internal dialogue. Only when exploration of your withdrawn state will your internal dialogue become consciously evident that you are, too, living as a powerless, apathetic victim or martyr that is also steeped in resistance.

As a martyr, you legitimately feel virtuous in your feelings, righteous to complain and calculate ways to manipulate others to get your own way. You see your entire life through a perspective that 'things constantly happen to me'. Being adept at getting others to feel sorry you help avoid being judged and criticized is the place of resistance. As a martyr, you may believe you 'deserve' better, which elicits others to sacrifice their own needs to care for you. The paradox is that martyrs expect less of themselves and find ways to avoid uncomfortable feelings or the experience of loss. You may seek safety from taking risks to avoid taking personal responsibility as you know others will also expect less from you.

As a martyr, you have the mastery to create a pity party by making a person or group of people seem unkind or insensitive to your needs. Telling your stories makes you feel interesting to others. You believe that you are communicating when in truth, your martyr is talking from your perspective and bias. It is based on your fears, your unresolved history, and your limiting beliefs. This power-play is quite an insidious and self-destructive use of your victim status. Essentially, you find value in gaining undivided attention and elicit sympathy for your plight, as any attention is better than no attention at all.

Chapter 6

Early Development Injuries Form the Martyr

Martyrs can be found in all families as no family is perfect. No matter what class, status, or background you come from, it is tragic yet natural that your primary caregivers failed you. It will be evident in the way you feel about yourself and your life. It is heart-breaking to bear that childhood, by its very nature, is damaging. Society and the environment also play their part to the detriment of the childhood developmental process. Malfunction is systemic in both families and society. Its negative effects are unconsciously passed down from one generation to the next.

Despite all the failings, these impressions and experiences impact our initial ideas about how we give and receive love. When relating, we can confuse fear with excitement and anxiety with passion. Sadly, we can believe that fear and anxiety is how relationships are supposed to feel because we have never experienced harmonious and loving relationships. Therefore, to make sense of those experiences, we would have made decisions about love, how to love and how to receive love from others.

The way we have learned to love is created by our early developmental injuries based on our childhood experiences. As our physiology and our mind are programed into a cycle of attachment and an addictive way of relating, which any of us will struggle to break free from. Viewed through the psychological lens, all our outer interactions are considered aspects of ourselves that we have unconsciously pushed out onto and into others, things, and life. We disowned aspects of ourselves from childhood because it was experienced as too painful.

Essentially, martyrdom is manifested from the experience of an unstable inner life. How you feel about yourself will depend on the degree you experienced the instability. You will have made fundamental decisions about how you feel about yourself – 'I'm not good enough' or 'there's something wrong with me'. Decisions and beliefs about life – 'I'm not in control,' 'life is scary', and decisions and beliefs about the world – 'the world is dangerous' or 'the world is unfair'. All your self-generated beliefs continue to influence your life, whether passed down inter-generationally, societally, or environmentally. Can you imagine how overwhelming it is for a child to cope with so much? Well, you are still coping with it, no matter what age you are now.

If your childhood were chaotic, traumatic, or inconsistent, along with having neglectful caregivers where you had received little or no empathy, as a child, you would have felt unmet, unseen, unheard, and misunderstood. You will have made relationships bonds through neglect, rejection, and shame. Essentially, a martyr is an adult with an undeveloped inner child. They are not broken, or in need of fixing, but they are deeply hurt and in need of considerable genuine love and care.

You may have felt from an early age that things were not right in your family. Things would have happened that you either did not trust or did not like, but deep down, you felt powerless as there was nothing you could do. Even if you wanted to run away, you could not because you were only little. As a child, we are always hoping and left waiting for the promise of things to get better.

Knowing something is wrong, you want it to be different. Hence, you try, despite your powerlessness, to change things in your limited capacity. You choose options and decide to either over-achieve so that praise and affirmation for your achievements become the compensation for perceived high self-esteem. Or you under-achieve, never taking opportunities to grow; therefore, your self-esteem is thwarted in the attempt that others continue to take care of you, or you care less and become oppositional, combative, and rebellious.

These multi-dimensional features are the under-developed parts of the Self that are all steeped in victimhood in their own unique way to a greater or lesser degree. In adult relationships, these present themselves as emotional immaturity that feeds a cycle of masochistic self-defeat or grandiosity, entitlement, tending to cause suffering in some way or another. All these facets are an abuse of power. You can feel stuck and powerless in adult relationships, but you will try to make the best of it due to how you have learned to bond and 'love'.

As a martyr, you sacrifice your authentic values and make intense and complex promises out of duty and loyalty. This is because you believe that being in the service of others' needs and wants is how you love and care for someone. This process becomes written into your core value system, beliefs, and principles which are generally held deeply in your unconscious. The subsequent conviction is you have no choice other than to suffer to feel loved and accepted.

Suffering from self-abandonment and self-neglect, the martyr or victim in you tries to run from the trouble and torment you suffer deep in your psyche. You may appear heroic, helping those in need to the detriment of your own, but in fact, you have not even considered you have needs of your own! Your heroic ability empowers your own wretched, meaningless, and miserable life, and you will be unable to receive love in its truest form.

As a martyr, you may unknowingly be seeking out persecution from the belief that you need to suffer and will never be happy. It is an unconscious fear of taking true personal responsibility and to experience joy, harmony, and authentic love. You are equally aiming at avoiding intimacy, companionship, and support and will predictably and unintentionally choose people who leave you feeling unworthy, disillusioned, disappointed, and mistreated.

As J.D. in childhood, you learned that it is not safe to express your true feelings and that others only value you when you are serving their needs. During your early development, you learned and believed to consider yourself unworthy of love and worthless as a person. Unfortunately, martyrdom is a role you identify with, and now, as an adult, you have become a full-blown martyr. Consequently, you are now prone to self-destructive, punishing, and self-defeating behaviors, learning to compensate for your emptiness by presenting your 'nice side' to others.

Your intention is always to be a good person, but you are bitter, resentful, confused, lost, and lonely inside. Attending to the needs of others while unintentionally denying your own, you are stuck in a cycle. You will fluctuate between acting helpless and leading to either a passive-aggressive stance, or your anger will get the better of you. Your rage will boil overdriving you to persecute those around you. Your outbursts are short-lived and soon turn into feelings of shame and guilt. This leads you to atone for them by doing good acts of service for the cycle to then continue.

Essentially, as a martyr, you have already been won over by the cycle of dysfunctional patterns of relating. This addictive cycle underpins the role you play in life and forms the persona you identify with. You will not only act out your dysfunctional attachments and ways of connecting, but you also wonder, '*Why is this always happening to me?*'. More importantly, you are playing out the martyr pattern internally, within yourself, all by yourself. You feel you must approach life from a survival instinct and gloss over the horrors. Your brain believes this is the best survival tactic to put up with any difficulties that life throws your way.

A significant contributor to keeping yourself stuck and powerless is your own internal negative self-voice. From absorbing the negative and critical things said to you in childhood, and the meaning you make from that is turned inwards and hence becomes learned self-talk. The saying goes, the biggest bully you will ever encounter is the voice in your own head. The inner critic of negative self-talk and harsh self-judgments is what keeps you stuck and powerless.

Having a tormentor as a companion living rent-free in your own head really brings you down. It can leave you feeling victimized, stressed, and fuelled with anxiety. Self-talk, self-blame, and rumination can take many forms. At times, it can seem reasonable and grounded, or it can be mean, cruel, and shaming. Nevertheless, you can feel its impact and its effects on your mind, body, life, and your relationships.

Negative self-talk is not only stressful, but it affects you deeply in damaging ways, limiting your ability to believe in yourself, thus holding you hostage to martyrdom. The capacity to see your potential is lowered, and opportunities to becoming a smartyr are thwarted.

As J.D., you uncompromisingly berate yourself into a powerless position as part of you tells yourself - 'I am worthless, and to feel valued and loved, I must meet the needs of others'. So, you will self-sacrifice and do whatever it takes to make things better, so you can say to yourself, 'I now feel good about myself'.

However, you continue to punish yourself and persist in telling yourself off. You say things like, 'I am not doing enough or making a big enough difference,' 'I am not good enough. Finally, feeling overwhelmed, resentful, bitter, and confused, you rage inside with statements such as 'It's not fair! What about me?' Punishing self-talk and worthless self-judgments begin to drive you once again back into your default position; thus, you allow the internal distortions to start all over again with a new internal and external drama and dialog.

Our behaviors and core beliefs originated from our impressions, interpretations, and experiences from our early family encounters and environment. Moving from these out-dated behaviors and negative self-talk is crucial to becoming a smartyr. Unconsciously acting out our history and early attachment traumas' reactions has become a 'life theme' that predisposes us by staying captivated by circulating this dysfunctional cycle.

You must become acquainted with the dance of distortions and dysfunctional internal dialog in your mind lasting minutes, hours, days, or even over your lifetime. When you choose to change the way you speak to yourself, it will help avoid you sacrificing your emotional and physical health and stress-related illnesses and diseases.

You can learn to catch yourself in negative self-talk and lessen the intensity and negative potency as you observe your language and effectively change it to a gentler approach. By pulling the camera back, you can take a much-needed reality check. Challenging the exaggeration of what you say and saying it out loud can help shift the perspective. Learning to speak to yourself like you are a supportive best friend or as if towards a child you deeply care about is a form of self-directed healing.

Chapter 7

The Cycle of Internal Dramas

Dr. Stephen Karpman, an American psychologist in Transactional Analysis in 1961, developed The Drama Triangle as a model to help us recognize our unconscious ways of relating.

Karpman's Drama Triangle illustrates the nature of power games, sometimes referred to as Mind Games or Game Playing. The power game is maintained by an unconscious and non-verbal agreement by all parties who play. Collusion, therefore, becomes the primary bond in which all players are complicit in keeping the drama alive out of the unknown desire to maintain familiarity, loyalty to feelings, core beliefs, and holding dysfunctional bonds.

The drama triangle impacts your present moment, your current relationships, and your daily life. The role you most relate to within the drama triangle is directly associated with your unhealthy childhood experiences, the dysfunctional circumstances from your life history, and the environment at that time.

Using an inverted triangle to map conflicted or drama–intense relationship dynamics, the triangle emphasizes the power in conflicts and the destructive and shifting roles we play. The model describes the outmoded ways we relate and present ourselves as victims, persecutors, or rescuers. All three roles of the persecutor, rescuer, and victim serve as an illusion of power and control.

The inverted triangle represents the persecutor and rescuer at the upper corners positioned parallel to each other to communicate the power positions toward the victim position at the triangle's apex. This is to substantiate superior feelings towards the 'one-down' position of the victim.

The drama triangle is not a definitive representation of our authentic Selves. It is a defended representation, an archaic replay for historical dysfunctional relationship dynamics that operate to keep us in an illusion of personal power. People play host to a primary position as their default. When they are hooked in and caught up in the cycle of internal dramas, all three positions are bound together to play out dysfunctional psychological dramas and games.

These interactions bond us into a poisonous co-dependent matrix that ultimately causes destruction and disappointment in all our relationships. Unknowingly we can all get caught in this cycle. If left unconscious, it is hard to escape. The end game is always negative when functioning, relating, and staying bonded within the cycle of internal dramas.

Whichever role you adopt or identify with most will misguidedly keep you disconnected from true intimacy and the opportunity to embrace a new reality where positive feelings can be experienced.

Firstly, you will unintentionally deny your true feelings. Then you will deny the feelings in others because of the perpetuated fixed role you play in the triangle. The act of denial is to keep you distanced and walled off from others - their loving connections and positive opportunities that present themselves to you. This is a rather unhealthy way to stay with the familiar misery of your life that you have made your reality.

These impressions tend to be your entry point into the drama triangle, reinforcing all your subjective experiences as an adult. It is an unfortunate attempt to keep yourself safe with the familiar, feel important, and feel special. This stance and attitude keep you in a place of shaming, blaming, and manipulative behavior, along with various addictions, chaos, and of course, the addiction of the drama itself. Your default role then becomes the strong part of your identity. You will have your own particular way of being, seeing, and reacting to the people around you and your environment.

Your feelings and beliefs are expressed by personal attitudes such as arrogance, denial, helplessness, etc., and behaviors such as depression, addiction, manipulations, scapegoating, incest, and abuse, and even kindness, over-caring, over consideration, and too much giving.

Your role in the internal cycle of dramas shows how conflict arises within you and the people around you. It demonstrates how you project the feelings you have about yourself that you do not like or would prefer to disown, and therefore push onto and into others. These modes of relatedness, or dramas, as Karpman states, are played out without any real awareness and is experienced as if it is happening to you in real-time.

You fluctuate with your feelings continuously simply because you are human. You will move around the triangle, automatically rotating through all the positions playing out the dysfunctional roles and negative interactions. For instance, if your life position resides in the victim, you may become angry at times towards the persecutor's abusive behavior, shifting you temporarily into the persecutor role to express your rage. Another example could be the persecutor may become guilty at the barrage of their abuse and therefore flip into the rescuing role to ease their guilt. Or the rescuer may become tired of giving so much that they may flip into a victim position to express their worthlessness. You can act out these roles in a matter of seconds, minutes, hours, or many times during the day or even over a lifetime. Although you move positions, you will fall back into your default position and start the game all over again with the main aim to defend and maintain your position.

The 1962 award-winning play by Edward Albee, 'Who's afraid of Virginia Wolfe', was adapted to film in 1966, which starred Elizabeth Taylor and Richard Burton. It showcases a classic example of the drama triangle in action and the painful psychological games being acted out between the married couple. Power games occur as they interchange between 'I'm OK, and You're not OK' and 'You're OK, and I'm not OK'. As soon as there is a power imbalance where one feels inferior and the other superior, the drama triangle becomes activated. The victim depends on a rescuer, rescuers yearn for a victim, and the persecutor needs a scapegoat; essentially, all the roles are rooted in victimhood and are unconscious to each role.

In families, the deeper that one or more family members are steeped in destructive behaviors, the bigger the family drama will become. In better functioning families, subtle versions of the drama triangle remain prevalent but are activated less dramatically. For instance, the persecutor (or abuser) is replaced by a dominant partner who has an agreeable partner going along with their lead. Subtle versions of the game, or the cycle of internal dramas, continue to be played out and becomes clear when significant stressful situations happen in the family. So, whether you are a full-blown martyr or a functioning martyr, it remains vital that you know the unconscious patterns that drive your life.

The primary learning for self-mastery is to learn your position and game on the triangle and to know when and how to exit it. You cannot leave the drama triangle until you recognize the part you play in the first place. Therefore, understanding how the three roles interchange will help you identify the emotional costs involved. It is essential to grasp how you have conformed to the roles to determine more positive and less destructive interactions with others and yourself.

No matter your default position, the victim role is where you inevitably end up as all roles are misguided in victimhood! The cycle of drama is essentially a cycle of contempt, shame, and abandonment. All those who play have an unconscious drive to prove they are the biggest victim. In each role, you are trying to prove you are right from your perspective even though the roles are pathological, negative, and ultimately damaging. If you find you are acting out as little as 10% of the drama cycle and when in a trusting relationship, it will be good enough, as no actual harm is caused to the relationship, especially if done with awareness.

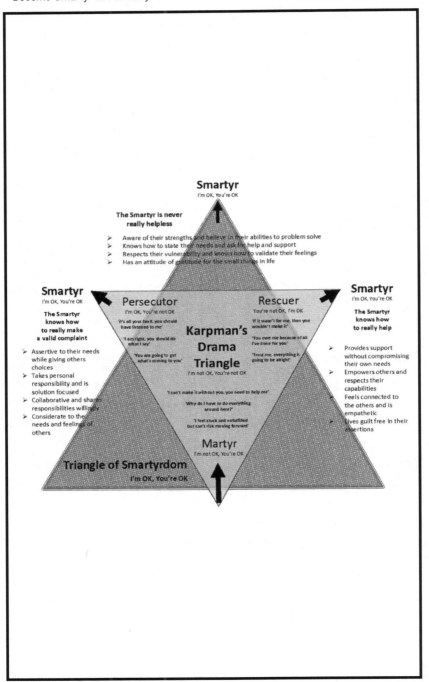

The following table outlines the different roles and how each position sees and presents itself

Rescuer	Persecutor	Victim
Who are you		
You are kind, caring, generous and have an abundance of goodwill, and make excuses for your high moral ground	You are condescending, controlling, and malicious and make excuses for your wrath	You are anxiety-driven, self-pitying, and complaintive and make excuses for staying stuck
You need to help others even when not asked to assert your power	You need to be in control and use verbal and physical force to assert your power	You need others to help solve your problems and keep you safe to assert your powerlessness
You find someone to be judgemental about to fix them to feel important and valued	You find someone to blame and complain about in order to stay angry and self-righteous	You find someone to blame and punish others to stay submissive and passive-aggressive

Rescuer	Persecutor	Victim
Why you do it		
To strive for value and appreciation from others	To strive to sustain your one-up position	To strive to get others to help you
To compromise attending to your own needs	To compromise your personal happiness and healthy relationships	To compromise your personal growth
To prove you are needed, and things cannot be done without you	To prove you are right to yourself and others	To prove you are at the mercy of everyone and everything

Rescuer	Persecutor	Victim
What you do		
You act dependable and capable as you rescue others from themselves	You act as an attacker and take all rights and give others none	You act helpless and powerless as you play the 'yes, but' game
You over-identify with other people's problems and try to solve them in order to stay in the role of the dominant person	You deal with threats, new ideas, and conflict with anger to stay in the role of the dominant person	You feed off the beliefs of the perpetrator and rescuer and stay stuck in your victimhood to stay in the role of the dominant person
You sustain your one-up position with a false sense of superiority by acting unselfishly to help others	You sustain your one-up position with a false sense of superiority by keeping people in denial	You sustain your one-down position with a false sense of inferiority by feeling sorry for yourself

Rescuer	Persecutor	Victim
What you say		
'If it wasn't for me, then you wouldn't make it.'	'It's all your fault; you should have listened to me.'	'I can't make it without you; you need to help me.'
'You owe me because of all I've done for you'	'I am right; you should do what I say.'	'Why do I have to do everything around here?'
'Trust me, everything is going to be alright.'	'You are going to get what's coming to you.'	'I feel stuck and unfulfilled but can't risk moving forward.'

Rescuer	Persecutor	Victim
What you fear		
You fear having no sense of belonging and will end up alone	You fear experiencing your vulnerability	You fear you won't make it in life
You fear you don't matter and have no importance in the lives of others	You fear feelings of powerlessness and becoming a victim	You fear your potential for self-generated power
You fear feeling guilty if you're not making a difference or doing enough	You fear feeling worthless	You fear change and growing up

Rescuer	Persecutor	Victim
What you believe		
I'm OK, but not until you're OK	I'm always OK, but you're not OK	You're OK, but I'm not OK
If I love someone enough, then I will be loved in return	The world is hard and mean, therefore I must be ruthless so I will survive	There is someone stronger and more capable to help me
I am needed; therefore, I must self-sacrifice my own needs to make it better	It's everyone else's fault, and I can see the truth, and others deserve what they get	I am intrinsically damaged and incapable

Rescuer	Persecutor	Victim
What you really don't know		
The world is unsafe, and I am powerless	The world is dangerous, and I am powerless	The world is resourceful, and I am powerful
I defend against feelings of guilt and shame by making my needs irrelevant	I defend against feelings of shame by using shame to keep others in their place	Shaming others into helping me is a defense against taking personal responsibility
When my help is not needed, I feel rejected and abandoned	Condemning others defends me against feeling shame and my intensified internal self-condemnation	When challenged, I use rage or my goodness to defend my inadequacies and feelings of shame

Your archaic acting out can stop! Your cycle of internal dramas will cease to exist! Once you have adopted the concepts and garnered the book's learnings, you will shift towards the smartyr position and away from your martyr position. Firstly, you need to be kind to yourself, and over time you will become your own best friend. When you become aware that your negative patterns of behaviors and the reasons for staying safe no longer work for you, it provokes personal and spiritual growth.

Becoming a smartyr is a calling from your soul. It wants to create true meaning in life. Curiosity and a yearning to understand, it motivates you to address your unresolved pain. When your pain is so great, you become a willing and active participant in the softening of your defenses because you want to discover that there must be a better way to live.

Growing and moving away from the drama triangle and becoming a smartyr can be challenging, depending on your intention. It is usually when a life crisis or a juncture in your life makes you realize that your unconscious programming influences the functioning patterns that no longer serve you.

To change power games and deeply embedded dynamics, first, you must begin to assert yourself. This will feel risky, as the people around you will feel threatened as you reform your position. They will accuse your assertions as persecutory. Your authenticity will be challenged by others. Their unconscious aim is to steer you back into the familiar place they need you to be in so they can maintain their role with you.

Paradoxically, it is the persecutory position that will help you leave the drama triangle. You will learn to sit with the discomfort of being perceived as the antagonist while subtle changes internally and externally begin to occur for the greater good.

However, do not be fooled into thinking you have exited the triangle; you may have just traded your default position for another! For instance, you may find yourself having moved from the victim life position to the rescuing life position. A game-free life aims to live authentically and no longer be an acting participant in the drama triangle.

Are You Ready?

If you are ready all the time,
you don't have to be ready

Chapter 8

Are You Ready to Grow Your Edges?

By no means are we implying that you need to change anything in your life. You may already live a fulfilled life, and you may be reading this book because you are merely curious. We understand if you would rather stay with the familiar.

You may also be reading this book because you are considering growing your edges and potentially inviting change to take place and embracing the beauty and idea of uncertainty.

Life is boring when nothing changes. We are hardwired to create meaning and grow our edges. You may choose to stay with what feels safe even though you may not be living a fulfilling life. However, life is all about change and growing your edges, and if that does not happen, then nothing changes.

Change happens as you step out of your place of familiarity. Not knowing what you will find and unable to control the outcome is like being in no man's land walking towards a shadowy figure. You may feel alone and vulnerable because the terrain is unpredictable, uncertain, and unfamiliar.

Take time to check in with yourself and assess your levels of boredom, stress, fear, and any uninterestingness. As you work through this book, we want you to slow down, look back, look within and notice what you find. Examine how you feel about your life and take time to process those thoughts. If you fail to do that, you will not develop the resilience, adaptability, and courage to grow your edges.

You will only be met with apprehension, trepidation, and fear and get caught up in a never-ending cycle or loop of paralysis. Your external world will remain as a projection of your internal state. What you think about becomes your reality which effectively creates your personality, and again, nothing changes. You stay stagnant, just pushing your dysfunction out into your world.

You may find something in your life that needs changing. You might lack motivation, or you feel a sense of unhappiness for some part of your day. You may feel blocked and frustrated in certain areas of your life, and no matter how much you try, you are not getting the results you want.

You may also notice that others seem to be changing, growing, and moving forward in their life. Noticing these observations may motivate you to re-evaluate your life, knowing that change will be more beneficial in the long run.

Real change happens from within. It comes from a desire to want more and to be more than you are. It is the built-in natural motivation and willingness to do an activity to reach one's goals to achieve a feeling of personal satisfaction and fulfill your dreams.

This is intrinsic motivation. Our focus is aimed at your intrinsic motivation. It is the driver that actively directs you towards your internal growth, to raise self-awareness, amass self-knowledge, and enhance your self-esteem. Your overall self-image improves, you begin to feel good about yourself, along with a sense of matured self-confidence and life abundant with quality relationships.

As people, we intrinsically know what is best for us. As mentioned earlier, you do not have active control over your unconscious because it operates out of your awareness. Your unconscious works independently from the conscious mind. It fools you into believing that you are making conscious choices. However, there are unconscious processes that influence your life without you knowing. It manages your life more than you realize.

What is Growing Your Edges?

You know, on some level, whether you choose to change or not, choices and decisions about your life are constantly being made and not always made by you. Change naturally happens all around you. Change is a struggle. It is uncertain; it is a challenge. You will need to open yourself up to internal exploration and learn to see things differently. You can view change processes as an opportunity to learn new skills, develop different attitudes and explore your capabilities. And this is what growing your edges is.

So, how do you grow your edges? Remember, you already have the qualities and attributes of a smartyr mindset already loaded in, lying dormant, waiting to emerge. Growing your edges is an active process that requires deliberate discipline on your part for change to happen. However, for things in your life to change, you need to become accountable for your actions. You will need to make choices and decisions that can be broken down into smaller segments and practiced feeling more manageable. When tiny changes occur, significant change happens.

Change is to make or become something different from what it is now or what it was in the past. It is fundamental human nature to resist change, especially a drastic one. The reality is the only constant thing is change. If you fear change and avoid making decisions, life will decide for you because life is change.

The seasons change, trends change, weather changes, and even your moods change; change is all around you in your external world. Change is either natural or reactive. Natural change occurs routinely in the ordinariness of your life, whereas reactive changes happen as a reaction to societal or environmental factors.

Remember, life is change, but your transformation will depend on your level of intention and motivation and not depend on just wishing for things to change. Therefore, no-one's personal transformation is immediate as it takes commitment, deliberate discipline, consistency of thought, and a compassionate disposition.

This book will be a gentle in-road to reveal some of your limiting beliefs that fuel your environment for martyrdom. You grow your edges towards smartyrdom when you become curious. With that curiosity lies an endless array of possibilities and opportunities. As your reality changes, you will unconsciously follow your heart and intuition and attract information that encourages your growth. You will honor the burning desire within and start thinking and imagining what and how you want your future to be. You will realize that you can choose to remain a victim of your history no longer or continue to be defined by your circumstances.

Chapter 9

Intrinsic Change

Intrinsic change is change within oneself – an inward movement towards internal satisfaction. Intrinsic change is less tangible and can be harder for you to notice and personally engage with if you are not connected to your feelings about change.

Firstly, how do you feel about change? Change is inevitable. Change is a process that encompasses the transition from one state, stage, or phase to another. Intrinsic change should not be confused and classified as an end goal or an event that occurs at a single point in time. Embracing change is a process and committing to change and the goals implemented along the way are what make the difference.

The experience of intrinsic change will stir feelings in you. As people, we naturally experience resistance to change even though change provides the ideal opportunity to work through and explore resistances and challenge our comfort zone. Your intentions around change are a perfect time for self-reflection, introspection, and consideration.

The transitions of change are strongly associated with the process of grief. Most of you will not resist change per se; what you will resist is the inconvenience and loss associated with what you have become attached to and with what is familiar. So essentially, when change happens, you will naturally experience a sense of loss.

You may know something in your life needs changing, like a job or career or the development of self-mastery. Change can also be conveniently avoided, denied, and procrastinated against even when you know that particular change or development needs to happen even when it is desired.

Intrinsic change requires self-compassion because change and the feelings associated with the process are directly linked to grief and loss. That can feel destabilizing and can make you feel like your life is out of control and uncertain. Unfortunately, feelings of grief and loss are a great motivator to kill your opportunities, spiral you into procrastination and self-defeating behavior!

By its very nature, humans fear change, and you will experience a change in your own unique and individual way. Change can have an effect on your self-esteem. It could make your life feel meaningless, intolerable, and lack purpose, as it can be hard to bear the ambivalent feelings associated with the challenges of transitions.

Even a chosen change or a natural positive one can feel overwhelming. Changes that bring about something good for you will also have an element of loss intertwined with the experience, despite even feelings of excitement. You could still feel apprehensive, fearful, doubtful, sad, relief or even confused. Once you realize that change is inevitable, whether you choose to change or it is thrust upon you, it is natural for a myriad of emotions to surface in association with loss.

By understanding and appreciating that change is closely related to the experience of loss, you can then allow natural feelings and emotions to surface, such as sadness, depression, worry, or anxiety. Recognizing and then managing these emotions through the transitions of intrinsic change will require self-care and patience to deal with them beneficially.

If you become a victim of your loss, it is essentially impossible to process and complete the cycle of grief. If, for example, you get stuck in the phase of letting go, you may actually become trapped as a victim of circumstance. This state of mind can lead to you to adopt the identity of a martyr spiraling you into a state of disappointment, self-pity, anger, sadness, depression, anxiety, and feeling a loss of a sense of Self. In other words, you forget who you are.

Once you have unconsciously and unknowingly adopted a martyrs identity, you will develop unhelpful thinking styles and behavior and say to yourself, 'This shouldn't be happening to me. I can't cope. I'm a failure. I'm a loser.' These counter-productive statements can impact and affect your close relationships, especially at a time when the support of your family and friends is essential. You may add, 'I'm not good company at the moment. Who wants to spend time with me while I'm feeling like this? Why don't my friends want to spend time with me?' The more you make statements such as these, the more reactive you will become and miss the opportunity to manage intrinsic change positively.

The essential nature of feeling like a victim and living in a state of martyrdom is your lack of insight and self-awareness. As a smartyr, you become open and willing to explore the predicaments of change and loss. So, to avoid falling victim to the vicious cycle, you need to decide to do something; you either choose to stay in this state or decide to move out of it. It is as simple as that. Making a decision requires taking responsibility for your internal experience of loss. Managing how you respond over time to change rather than reacting to change will decide how you experience the journey of change as a positive or negative one.

This book is about intrinsic change and personal transformation with the potential to develop into a smartyr. It would help if you gave yourself time to grow your edges and experience the pain of change and loss. This time will allow you to move through to a place of surrender, flow, and acceptance and for extrinsic change to become evident in your life.

Being open about your emotional reactions and sharing the way you feel with those close to you or with a professional will help clarify what is happening to you. Support of this kind will engender some relief and comfort and give you a different perspective. The emotions you attribute to change makes the difference in experiencing change as either good or bad, tolerable, or intolerable.

Pull back and observe yourself as if you are watching a film of your thoughts, feelings and behaviors. Taking an internal inventory, you could consider asking yourself or journaling answers on the following page to questions such as:

* Why am I even reading this book?
* Do I even want to change who I am?
* Am I curious about myself?
* What do I feel about myself when I look in the mirror?
* Why am I feeling like this?
* Is this a familiar feeling?
* Do I even want to feel this way?
* What is it that I can do to intrinsically change how I feel?

At this point, you can begin to see the limiting beliefs you hold true about yourself. These beliefs are the foundation to personal outcomes concerning your growth and the change and the losses associated with adopting a new smartyr identity. The insights garnered as you journey through this book will support you to cope with the experience of change and loss as you develop a unique and smartyr identity.

Journaling
Insights - Thoughts - Reflections

Chapter 10

Experiencing Resistance

Now, are you ready to make a choice? Grow or not grow, change, or not change, evolve, or not evolve, choose smartyrdom over martyrdom? However, choosing to make a positive change can feel scary because it is human nature to be averse to unfamiliar, uncertain, and unpredictable.

Making changes can lead you to opposition and resistance but realizing that you have the power to choose. By making choices gives you the ability to create whatever you want in your life despite your resistance. While reading this book, you may understandably feel resistant. Are you sure you are connecting to a place of choice first? Have you chosen to read this book because you actively want to make change happen in your life?

We are sure you can find many reasons to stay where you are to avoid experiencing uncomfortable feelings or emotions. So, despite your good intentions and determination to become smartyr, moving away from the surroundings of familiarity is not always easy. Slipping back into your old patterns of behavior is normal and expected when you are practicing something new. Your unconscious negative thoughts and dysfunctional beliefs are causing you to experience this resistance and disconnect from a place of making a choice to change.

It is professionally researched that, unfortunately, for us humans, negativity sticks like Velcro, and positivity sticks like Teflon. Evolutionary survival required our pre-wired brain to respond negatively to our surroundings to keep us alert to our immediate environment's dangers. When you stress or have a negative thought, it associates your negative thoughts as a real danger, and you do not know what to do. Choice seems unavailable to you.

Even though we no longer fear the pending doom of a fearsome saber-toothed tiger, most of us lean towards negative thinking. Unfortunately, the resistance associated with the threat of change cannot be rationalized, as our brain gets tricked into imagining and believing the threat or danger is real.

Given those circumstances, your desire and motivation to change your life can be a challenge. Consequently, moving away from your victim life position into a smartyr life position is no mean feat. Allow for relapses from time to time as you meet these resistances. You may experience feelings of push and pull, such as 'I want it, don't want it', or 'I'm not ready', etc. Do not let uncooperative oppositional behaviors discourage you against any suggestions that you do not have the will or desire to move forward.

Unless challenged, these negative structures will continue to replay like a tape recording on a constant loop - unconsciously directing the course of your life. The impressions left in the auto-play mode keep the programming and behaviors running, reinforcing your belief systems for good or ill. This state develops into a template where your identity and sense of Self is formed and expressed. Resistance, therefore, becomes entrenched.

For example, you may carry the negative belief that you are bad and selfish because you want to speak up about how you feel.

This subconscious negative belief associated with the threat of criticism, and the lack of ever having been adequately validated when you were little, reinforces feeling blocked and stuck. These negative impressions maintain your resistance to taking action and feeling a lack of motivation to want to, know how to, or have the desire to create any positive change.

The above is one typical example of how negative core beliefs conditioned into the subconscious are manifested by early childhood, become an inevitable resistance in your current reality. Suppose you have unknowingly developed a martyr mindset based on your early impressions. Unfortunately, this mindset will thwart your best intentions and interfere with having progressive experiences and opportunities in life.

Practice and commitment are everything. When you get your conscious mind out of the way, it allows for your subconscious mind to be open to new suggestions for positive change. Especially when engaging in our read–aloud smartyr self-hypnosis. At this point, you can re-program new and positive affirmations and give your creative mind, or smartyr mind, new instructions to aid the flow towards personal transformation. The subconscious mind is where all your creativity sits, ready to help you once you can get past your resistance. You will become the cause of your life rather than the effect of it.

We want you to live your life the way you want and become your natural Self, if you approach this book and its exercises without the effort of 'trying'. To action them indicates you have an open mind to approach the work without a doubt because 'to try' is another form of resistance and shows you have doubt in your belief that this book can change your life.

Living takes effort, whilst dying is the natural default. You can move your life in a positive direction. It is your choice that makes all the difference. In the film Shawshank Redemption, Andy Dufresne said to his fellow inmate Red: "Life comes down to a simple choice: you get busy living, or you get busy dying." Are you ready to get busy living, or do you choose a life half lived?

You are embarking on the process of intrinsic change, a journey of growth, maturation, self-mastery, self-realization, and ultimately, smartyrdom.

Chapter 11

Having Choices and Making Decisions

When it comes to choosing, it may seem that the word choice and decisions have the same meaning, but when it comes to making an intrinsic change in your life, there is a difference. To make a change in your life is not just a simple matter of just making a decision; firstly, you must choose to make a change. However, your resistance and unconscious blocks are likely to make you unaware that the opportunity and freedom to choose is available to you.

From our psychological perspective, when you were little and growing through your developmental stages, you did not experience much free choice, as your parents did most of that for you. Imagine how lovely it is for a child to experience their parent, offering them an opportunity to choose which pudding they want. The internal dialogue of the child is 'Oh wow, I can decide!'. The excitement of this experience elicits delight in the freedom to choose. The child begins to value its assertiveness, which develops their confidence, raises self-esteem, and encourages self-control when they experience a world of endless 'no's, do's, don't.'

In normal development, if the child chooses rice pudding, it naturally gives up on the vanilla ice cream. They imagine the ice cream and can let it go as they settle for the rice pudding. They can then fully engage with their decision and enjoy it. Effectively, by making a choice, the child goes through the critical process of accepting their choice and grieves what effectively is left behind – the ice cream.

Unfortunately, as an adult, you may find you struggle in life when the process of choosing and deciding has not been practiced enough, learned, and integrated. The child must choose, as the parent will not hang around too long; so, it does. It chooses something or nothing at all, or it picks rice pudding.

Let's say the child struggles to choose yet decides on rice pudding. Instead of engaging with the rice pudding and enjoying it, they feel they are missing out on the ice cream. Essentially, they have not learned to grieve the loss of something. Everything the child chooses while growing up represents something they do not choose. In everything they get, there is something they do not get. They eventually learn life works this way. The child learns to value adaptability, which lends itself to developing their independent spiritual value system where balance, fairness, and tolerance are cultivated.

Choice is when you can select from two or more options and have the freedom and the opportunity to make a choice. Visiting the place of choice is what connects you to the place of deciding. You are making choices and decisions day in, day out. Even choosing not to decide is a decision. Letting something go and allowing 'life' to decide is a choice. You unconsciously make choices and decisions automatically and mostly without thinking.

Although you continually make conscious choices, you are also regularly making unconscious decisions. It does not help that there is an undeniable barrage of information and choice imposed on us in society today, which leaves us in a state of suspense and procrastination. Even buying a cup of coffee has become an overwhelming decision-making process because your future hinges on the choices you make now.

For example, imagine you want a coffee. You have the right, power, and opportunity to choose; you need to decide which coffee. Suppose you select a cappuccino, added to that, you must also choose from small, regular, or grande! Let's say you decide on a flat white as the cup is standard, and so now you feel relief, as your decision has been made easier. But now, you face the dilemma if you want the creaminess of a flat white or if you really prefer the froth of the cappuccino. Now, along with the added time pressure, the cashier is eagerly waiting as the queue builds behind you. You are now in a state of frenzy and having an internal meltdown at having to make a quick decision in the hope you have made the right choice. Now imagine that same process when you are faced with real-life choices and making decisions.

So how do you cope with this onslaught? The result is easy; just make a choice; you will get a coffee. To decide will benefit your nervous system. But you may feel pressured because you fear the negative results. The subliminal expectations are, you must make the right choice to keep up with modern society trends for fear of imagining that you are missing out on something.

Another strain is getting caught up and stressing over a lot of things that really do not matter. As a smartyr, it does not matter what decision you make or what you may or may not be missing out on. What matters most to you is what you do after you make your decision. Once you choose, as a smartyr, you will flow with your choice, trusting that any mistake has the potential to turn out to be no mistake at all. As a smartyr, you have come to value openness, confidence, spontaneity, and opportunities.

The Victim is not really as helpless as they feel

-

The Rescuer is not really helping

-

The Persecutor does not really have a valid complaint

Claude Michel Steiner – Psychotherapist

The Smartyr

"Knowing others is intelligence; knowing yourself is true wisdom Mastering others is strength; mastering yourself is true power"

Lao Tzu, Tao Te Ching

As a smartyr, I believe my purpose in life is to develop more consciousness, freedom, and order as I believe that is the fundamental expression of my creativity and an affirmation of my self-worth. I do not believe luck happens to me; instead, I believe in being the cause and creator of my life rather than its effect. I work on noticing chance opportunities to develop my skills that aid the free expression of my creativity.

Despite the ordinariness of life, I do not feel the need to chase anything as I already make an interesting life. I adopt a positive mentality and enjoy the rewards of my autonomy as I feel in control of my life. My smartyr Self feels successful as I make decisions based on listening to my intuition, which restores my faith and trust in the world. I use my time effectively. I do not have a good day; I make an intention to have a good day, filling it with productivity, moving conscientiously towards reaching my goals. My aspirations and gratitude keep me busy, which provides a positive force in my life.

I view challenges as an opportunity for learning and growth as the true test of my resiliency is when life does not go my way. When I experience feelings of sadness, anger, and disappointment, I keep a good perspective with the flexibility for growth and wisdom. I focus on what I can do and am confident there are many solutions and possibilities for every problematic encounter.

I embrace people, new ideas and have practiced the art of allowing others to support me with my achievements. However, having the wisdom to know my limitations signifies relief in me, and that hope still exists because the difference lies in my motivation to know when to stop doing something. Understanding the difference between quitting and letting go is, I quit when I stop giving my 100%, but when I let go, I know my 100% is not worth it.

Living blame-free, I am virtuous and diligent at being aspirational and inspirational. I take pleasure in seeing others grow. I naturally engage with people, enjoy relationships, and feel the value of providing attention to others' plight with compassion and empathy. I approach life through a perspective that 'success is possible for all'. And I have the mastery to positively create, making a person or group of people adopt kindness and sensitivity to their needs and to the needs of others. Essentially, my mindset is that I deserve to be content in the spirit of harmony, and I feel rewarded, and experience a sense of belonging".

Chapter 12

The Smartyr

A smartyr has a positive attitude which creates their reality

The Life and Values of the Smartyr

As a smartyr, you are prepared to face one of life's most difficult challenges, which is the practice of honesty. In other words, you are ready to take a good hard look at yourself to procure a growth mindset with a desire to evolve and create the life you want.

This is not about becoming self-absorbed, self-aggrandizing, conceited, or exaggerating your self-importance and power; it is actually a self-effacing process. For this reason, with the humblest approach, your self-directed focus is primarily invested in your self-mastery and maturity.

Charged by curiosity to motivate and deliberately challenge you, you campaign for a firm sense of individuality and for an autonomous and harmonious life. You do not strive for perfection because you know that will get in the way of achieving your goals.

You have come to value humility and recognize it as a strength. You have learned to accept and appreciate that all mishaps are learning opportunities. Because you have committed to the art of mental toughness to know your strengths and weaknesses, you are willing to grow and develop your resilience across multiple domains in life.

Emotional Intelligence and Emotional Literacy

Becoming a smartyr naturally enhances an attitude of gratitude and acceptance for what is. By having cultivated an open-mind and non-judgemental attitude, you want to influence others' growth. You become invested in others, becoming the best version of themselves.

You manage your strong emotions and impulses and focus on developing a compassionate mindset as you no longer see yourself as a victim. Instead, you think about feelings because you understand that your thoughts and feelings impact and influence others. You can quietly observe yourself and reflect on those observations. This enables you to see what is happening, just below the surface of what might really be going on. This allows you to identify the reasons behind your emotional reactions and your behavior toward people and the situation.

You do not hold another's emotions hostage; you can forgive and forget. You can move on and give yourself a chance to heal. You study your behavior; you identify your triggers. You have cultivated the habits you need to successfully keep your emotions in balance.

As emotions are experienced instinctively in the body, most people cannot control how they feel at any given moment. As a smartyr, you understand what you feel because you can recognize your own bodily sensations on an emotional level. As you are aware of your mind-body connection, you trust what your body tells you; therefore, you can identify and distinguish your emotions and feelings as separate from another.

As a smartyr, you recognize that you can manage your reactions to your feelings by giving yourself time to think and focus on your thoughts. Because you understand and appreciate how your thoughts contribute to the management of your feelings, you can use this awareness to remind you that your feelings are only fleeting. That being so, you can take a pause and allow yourself to think before speaking or taking action. This practice prevents you from becoming a slave to your emotions.

Taking a pause guides your intentions and goals with less impulsivity, hesitation, and uncertainty. Therefore, you never make any major or minor decision based on an emotionally charged moment. You give yourself time to think and have mastered a self-reflective process.

You are aware of the disempowering impact of rumination, catastrophizing, and wasting time on negative ideas and experiences. You can differentiate between thoughts and facts. By making the separation and neutralizing all negative self-talk and negative self-judgment, you can make decisions more positively and with more clarity.

Interpersonal Dynamics

You realize and understand not everyone is interested or ready to listen to what you have to say. Instead, you inspire the people around you and become aspirational as you lead by example. The by-product is you become a valued asset to society.

You find you are naturally attracted to people who aid your development and help you find new perspectives. You know you cannot fundamentally change people, so you except feedback and criticism. You reframe what you hear as a tool for personal growth.

Based on this, smartyrs are difficult to offend. You are by no means a robot because words and actions can also be upsetting for you. However, you have built up a certain level of resilience, detachment, and self-confidence that allows you to poke fun at yourself and brush off any negativity. It involves recognizing that you do not know everything, and you are open and willing to learn from others. You engage proactively with any challenges you encounter, as you are motivated to gain competence and trust in your self-belief.

As a smartyr, you have learned the art of small talk, you have developed how to tell a good story. You use anecdotes, facts, and ideas and bring stories to life. This way, you naturally find people interested in the things you say and what you do. You confidently share real-life examples because you know they will touch, inspire, and motivate others, which leads to deep and meaningful conversations.

Smartyrs enjoy commending others rather than diminish them. By contrast, you look for the good in them. You like to share specific praise and focus on nurturing others' potential. You have mastered the best way to inspire someone by extending a supportive hand and embracing people's diversity. When interacting, you avoid half-truths and make an authentic effort to talk and present information that does not get misinterpreted. This is a certified way to build trust with others.

Your inner structure is cultivated to safeguard you from emotional manipulation from people who are not suitable for you. You realize that there are darker aspects to everyone. You have learned to use your power with integrity. You remain aware that there are individuals who use manipulation, deception and abuse their power to pursue their goals at the expense of others. Overtime, smartyrs become good judges of character. They can distance themselves from those who try to bring them down.

As an established smartyr, you can sense and respond to others' needs and emotions yet remain unswayed when saying no and will not allow guilt to cloud your decisions. You assert your right to express your reasonable expectations to others. You know you are not responsible for others, and others are not responsible for you.

Smartyrs understand the importance of an apology. Saying sorry can be the most difficult word to say to others and to yourself. You know that saying sorry is not an admission to being wrong; it means that you value the relationship more.

One of the main hallmarks of a smartyr is their empathic nature. You can see things through the eyes of another and from their perspective. You actively listen because you want to understand and avoid forming judgments. This allows you to relate to others from a compassionate viewpoint. It shows the level of sincerity and curiosity you have towards them. This leads to deeper connected relationships in business, in love, and in life.

As a smartyr, you know the importance of relaxation. You know when and how to relax because you do not need to understand every feeling and experience. You do not have to over analyze or dissect every event as it happens. You simply enjoy the moment when it is beneficial to do so. You believe not everything is always a challenge you must overcome.

You keep your commitments. Because as a smartyr, you realize that keeping your word establishes a strong reputation that gains you respect from others as a reliable and trustworthy person. You make yourself accountable for your obligations and duties and respond appropriately to your actions and behaviors.

Essentially, smartyrs have learned to build authority over who they are. You are aware the boundaries and limits that you set are not rigid, as you can change them by renegotiation. You can make yourself available to listen and are more attuned to be responsive to others with compassion.

Boundaries

Introducing boundaries ensures that you do not become overwhelmed by other people's demands or feel guilty for taking personal responsibility for setting limits. You have learned to manage yourself and other people effectively when negotiating appropriate boundaries. You understand you cannot like everyone, and not everyone will like you.

You know how to set boundaries. You appreciate this as the way to healthy relationships. You are more explicit with others about who you are, what you want, your beliefs, core values, and know how to set your limits. When you have mastered the fundamentals of internal and external boundaries, you feel the quality of being emotionally and mentally stable. This is about creating an environment where you protect your relationships by caring about the quality of them.

You know that having fostered the attributes of personal boundaries allows you to set limits and yet remain a loving and caring person. You can give and expect nothing in return. You can be selfless and think about others' wellbeing, but you are not boundaryless. So, psychologically speaking, boundaries are the invisible personal property lines that define who you are and who you are not.

Endowing boundaries is pertinent in all areas of your life as they define you as self-contained and distinct from others. Establishing personal boundary lines conserves your emotional energy, allows independent thinking and autonomy, and keeps your self-esteem intact.

Setbacks

You are resilient with realistic optimism because, as a smartyr, you have garnered the ability to withstand adversity and setbacks. You have stopped playing the 'what if' game as you have learned to overcome what you thought was once lost opportunities when really, you have allowed those mistakes to offer you new ideas and possibilities rather than dwell on the past.

With this strength, you get down to business quickly and create strategies to accomplish things. You are more intrinsically motivated to get things done based on your learning from past experiences. You understand that setbacks are impermanent, and any emotional pain will pass because you care for your own wellbeing.

As a resilient smartyr, this process allows you to bounce back and recover from traumatic or stressful events quicker as you cope adaptively with change, challenges, disappointments, and failures. You trust your flexibility and adaptability, and you view change as non-threatening. The strength of resilience empowers you to accept and adapt to situations as a way of you moving forward. Having cultivated and absorbed resilience as a character strength, it eventually becomes your natural tendency.

You may be resilient and secure in your work-life yet can be less resilient and insecure in your personal and private life. However, you will have cultivated enough self-awareness to realize that developing resilience is a personal process. You have learned to push past any initial discomfort to recognize that there are greater joys and satisfaction ahead.

Overall, you appreciate that resilience allows you to understand your thoughts and emotions, which is essential to know what you want for new insights and growth. Ultimately, it is a form of having deep self-respect, leading to your true wisdom that enhances your choices, decisions, and experiences.

Personal Values

Personal values, simply put, are the things that are important to you and are the compass that points you to your truths. Making a conscious effort to identify and live by smartyr values is vitally important because your personal values, good or bad ones, are an extension of yourself. They define you because they underpin all motivation, goal setting, and actions, whether they end up becoming positive or negative experiences.

Your personal values, good or bad, are innate within you and are subjective to your feelings and beliefs that operate in your unconscious that influences your behavior. Therefore, they are not deliberately chosen or selected; instead, they reveal themselves to you through your life experiences. This is the process of you raising consciousness, gaining insight, and developing self-awareness.

It is not enough to just talk about self-improvement; you need to explore your values because the benefits of knowing them can help you in a variety of ways at being a smartyr. However, sometimes we have no idea what we want or what our personal values really are. Deciding on smartyrdom will naturally direct you towards exploring your current personal values.

At the back of this book, we have supplied an extensive list of values you may want to consider. As you explore them, you will find many that resonate with you and see that there is a natural hierarchy in how you prioritize them. For instance, you may value kindness and compassion over fame and popularity.

Good values are intrinsic and are achieved internally, like humility and compassion. These qualities reflect reality and are authentic because they can be expressed immediately and are controlled by you. It is socially constructive because the people around you benefit from your authenticity.

Bad values, by contrast, rely on external events and lie out of your control. For instance, fame is a bad value because you cannot control who or how many people like you. Therefore, it is not immediate because it is driven by external requirements. It does not reflect reality because it engages you with the world as you wish it to be or by having to meet the unknown expected standards of others. It is socially destructive because it is an expression of your inauthenticity.

Having discovered them gives you the chance to evaluate and define them, supporting you to make any necessary changes in your life for more fulfilling experiences. Knowing them helps you find your purpose, achieve your objectives, make intelligent decisions, increase your confidence, and guide you through difficult situations by playing to your strengths and moral code.

Over time, some of your personal values will remain unchanged because you have made them the bedrock for your core values and moral principles. You may decide to change some of them as you mature, develop new outlooks and priorities, or when your life circumstances change.

Chapter 13

Smartyr's Route
to Sabotage

Ways to develop your smartyr Self is an experiential process where you will gain health, satisfaction, and self-esteem. However, the road to smartyrdom is also about accepting the short-term pain that goes with change. At times, expect feelings of inconvenience, sacrifice, or even deprivation. While you may find it a blurred experience and wonder if anything is changing at all, at times, you will have some defining moments.

Your experiences are likely to be small and slow at first. These experiences will eventually become integrated once you have stopped to reflect on your progress and evaluate where you were to where you find yourself now. Slowing down the process of going through this book is an excellent way to interrupt your automatic, habituated thoughts and patterns that can easily be missed in split-second occurrences. So, if you decide to take the road to become smartyr, it will require your commitment to stay focused.

Be realistic to the obstacles and resistance that may stand in your way to achieving your desired outcome. When you are ready and open to give up old habits, limiting beliefs, and patterns of behaviors, this book will change your life. Be realistic in assessing the amount of time it will take for the changes you need to accomplish and become integrated. Honesty in your assessment of how much needs to be changed is crucial; monitoring and evaluating how successful you are in making your lifestyle changes.

There are stages to goal setting if you are to be successful. Any new venture will require a level of commitment, courage, and a motivational drive. Usually, when you want something different, there is a sacrifice on your time or money and the people around you. Friends and family may see less of you, not only in time, but your emotional free attention is likely to be eaten up too. So, consider the fact others may not like it! Foresee these implications and have discussions with those who champion you the most, as they may need to re-evaluate their own life and routine to support you, the family, and themselves.

Sabotage by Others

It is important to be around people who will support your success and growth. Once you decide to become smartyr, it is crucial to understand that the people around you will be affected. People need you in a particular position in their lives. They have become accustomed to the familiar ebb and flow of relatedness with you. Any whiff of change in character or behavior can stir up a challenge in them. Their role with you is shaken, and unconsciously, feeling threatened, they may not know how to meet the change and relate differently with you. In turn, you may begin to relate differently to them.

While you may want to celebrate your ideas and share your learning, to stay on track, you may need to be aware of unconscious sabotage by those closest to you. Your success in becoming a smartyr will generate others' envious projections onto you and into you. Unwittingly, their gestures of goodwill and pride could be insidious attempts to bring you down to keep you the same or as you were.

As you change the game, a rift is created as you become unfamiliar, generating fear in them as they begin to feel left behind or left out. Feelings of guilt, either self-inflicted or imposed, may compromise your attempts to move forward. You may feel torn between staying loyal to your constellated position and your desire to set goals and change.

Not all people will resent you; some may genuinely wish to celebrate your success. But your growth can make some people feel inadequate, making them question their own abilities and making them face their own lack and unresolved pain of their past. Questions like 'Why is it others can do well when I remain trapped?' evokes feelings of envy and thoughts of 'Life is not fair.'

There is a difference between enemies and haters. Enemies blatantly bring you down, but haters do the opposite; they may validate you in front of everyone but steeped in envy, they insidiously sabotage your efforts. Secretly wishing to be you, they deny their capacity to drive their own success, and instead, they allow their envy to get the better of them. If this envy remains out of their awareness, negative feelings of anger, bitterness, and resentment, along with jealousy and sadness, get acted out, and they attempt to clip your wings. They may even get a kick out of derailing your goals, like when someone is goading you to have just one more drink when they know you are trying to cut down or stop. Or a sly remark is made to ridicule you, hoping that you will doubt yourself.

They look forward to spending time with you to make you feel bad about yourself. This is usually portrayed by being extra critical of your thoughts and actions. Some will act like they are never impressed. No matter how much you model your growth, they will try and 'one-up' you from the side-lines. And they can become defensive and angry when you start sharing your successes.

How will you ever succeed if you are the only stakeholder committed to your plan? While it may not be overtly intentional to get kicks out of derailing your goals, consider ways to protect yourself from sabotage. So, what are the signs to look out for when someone is trying to sabotage your road to smartyrdom?

* **Keep quiet** – People do not always need to know your plans, ideas, and aspirations straight away.
* **Only talk** to those interested in what you have to say or what you are doing. You will feel more supported.
* **Don't feel guilty** – Spending less time with others doesn't mean you love them any less. It's easy to feel bad when others start complaining you are not there for them in the usual way.
* **Set boundaries** – When you are in the company of others, it's ok to hold back from what you would naturally share. You are not disloyal or careless.
* **Be alert** – No matter how small the jibe might be, stay acute to what is happening around you.
* **Resist arguing** – If you find yourself being challenged, avoid confrontation. Don't become defensive and feel you should justify yourself or overly explain your reasons.
* **Be gentle with yourself** – It's easy to take things personally, especially when you care about the person.

Handle being bothered by their actions with love and compassion towards yourself.

* **Be compassionate** – Ask yourself, could they be saying this because:
  - They feel scared and insecure?
  - If I succeed, it means they have failed?
  - They have no idea what they just said (or did)?

If the answer to any of these is 'yes,' then think before delving into reacting unfavourably. Remember, most people are acting out unconsciously; they legitimately believe they are supportive!

Self–Sabotage

You are likely to self-sabotage if you do not discover your personal values. It is important to know what they are because your personal values guide all your constructive and destructive behavior. Knowing what they are, means you will have better control of them; otherwise, those values will control you. If you do not consider what they are or the fact that you even need them, you could sabotage your growth and development. Unevaluated personal values prime you to be reactive to life and circumstances rather than responsive. You end up making reckless decisions that are not aligned with you becoming a smartyr.

Chapter 14

Useful Road Map

The next part of this book focuses on where you are now, where you are going and how to get there.

On occasion, in our practice, we have found it helpful to use the Victim to Survivor to Thriver™ table by Barbara Harris Whitfield. The table below highlights a journey that needs to be taken when you are ready to become smartyr, not a martyr.

Where you are now	Where you are going	Where you want to be
Victim	**Survivor**	**Thriver**
Doesn't deserve nice things or trying for the "good life"	Struggling for reasons and chance to heal	Gratitude for everything in life
Low self/esteem shame/ unworthy	Sees Self as wounded and healing	Sees Self as an overflowing miracle
Hyper-vigilant	Using tools to learn to relax	Gratitude for a new life
Alone	Seeking help	Oneness
Feels selfish	Deserves to seek help	Proud of healthy self-caring
Damaged	Naming what happened	Was wounded and now healing
Confusion and numbness	Learning to grieve, grieving past ungrieved trauma	Grieving at current losses
Overwhelmed by past	Naming and grieving what happened	Living in the present
Hopeless	Hopeful	Faith in Self and life
Uses outer world to hide from Self	Stays with emotional pain	Understands that emotional pain will pass and brings new insights

Hides their story	Not afraid to tell their story to safe people.	Beyond telling their story, but constantly aware they have created their own healing
Believes everyone else is better, stronger, less damaged	Comes out of hiding to hear others and have compassion for them and eventually Self	Lives with an open heart for Self and others
Often wounded by unsafe others	Learning how to protect Self by share, check, share	Protects Self from unsafe others
Places own needs last	Learning healthy needs (See Healing the Child Within & Gift to Myself)	Places themself first, realizing that is the only way to function & eventually help others
Creates one drama after another	See patterns	Creates peace
Believes suffering is the human condition	Feeling some relief, knows they need to continue in recovery	Finds joy in peace
Serious all the time	Beginning to laugh	Seeing the humor in life
Uses inappropriate humor, including teasing	Feels associated with painful feelings instead	Uses healthy humor
Uncomfortable, numb, or angry around toxic people	Increasing awareness of pain and dynamics	Healthy boundaries around toxic people, including relatives
Lives in the past	Aware of patterns	Lives in the Now
Angry at religion	Understanding the difference between religion and personal spirituality	Enjoys personal relationship with the God of their understanding
Suspicious of therapists – projects	Sees therapist as a guide during projections	Sees reality as their projection and owns it
Needs people and chemicals to believe they are all right	Glimpses of self-acceptance & fun without others	Feels authentic & connected, whole
Depression	Movement of feelings	Aliveness

Smartyr Self Hypnosis

**Self-Awareness is the Key
to Self-Mastery**

Chapter 15

Smartyr Self-Hypnosis

Self-Awareness is the Key to Self-Mastery

Being in a trance or hypnotic state is one of the oldest of the medical arts. It is a psychological phenomenon and, unbeknown to most, is also a natural and healthy everyday occurrence. If you have no experience of hypnosis or meditation, then carry on reading further. It is beneficial if you read through this section before you begin to hone your practice. These sections will give you the necessary information you need to make a successful start on your journey of self-hypnosis.

A hypnotic state can look and feel like being asleep. Anyone can drift into a natural auto-pilot mode when simply going about their normal daily activities. You drift into 'the zone' or are 'in flow' or find yourself in a natural gaze that you become oblivious to your immediate surroundings. It is neither normal sleep nor a state of wakefulness. Being in a hypnotic state is somewhere in between the two.

Traveling, listening to music, engrossed in TV or film, reading, engaging in physical exercise, housework, or concentrating on any focused activity can all induce a self-hypnotic state. These are all a constant source of natural subliminal suggestibility. Therefore, hypnosis is simply the feeling of focused attention, whether you are actively practicing it or not.

The natural hypnotic state is known as a hypnoidal state, which refers to light hypnosis with some sleep qualities without having experienced any formal therapeutic interaction. The qualities of hypnoidal sleep states are known as hypnogogic and hypnopompic states. It is the process of near awakening and near sleep.

Hypnogogic state is the stage we pass through as we process our waking consciousness into a state of sleep. Hypnopompic is the stage we pass through as we wake up, moving from sleep to being consciously awake. These hypnogogic and hypnopompic states are both highly suggestible moments.

When you go to a professional hypnotherapist, they will actively engage you in hypnosis to help you with a particular concern. They will use deliberate suggestibility to bypass the Critical Factor. This is the gatekeeper of your mind; it is the gateway between the conscious and subconscious mind. Once bypassed, autosuggestion is embedded, and reprogramming occurs.

It is important to be reassured that you have the power to accept or reject any suggestions from entering the subconscious mind. You also can snap out any trance-like state at any given moment at any time. Remember, all deliberate hypnosis is effectively a form of self-hypnosis which means the control is always with you. The hypnotherapist is simply the facilitator to help you focus on embedding a new idea into the unconscious.

Chapter 16

Differences Between Hypnosis and Meditation

Hypnosis is delivered in the form of suggestions and aims toward achieving an outward change. Meditation, however, emphasizes achieving a specific internal state. Both meditation and hypnosis activate the left pre-frontal lobe, linked to positive emotions, autonomy, and happiness. This activation affects the brain's alarm center, known as the amygdala, reducing the harmful effects of stress. Effectively, hypnosis can be experienced like or different from meditation, depending on your preference, mindset, and previous knowledge and experience of either process.

Either way, both methods need to quiet the mind. Shockingly, the psychological present moment is experienced in a window of only about three seconds. If you notice how much chatter goes on at any given moment in your mind, you will find it a very noisy place; it always wants to be elsewhere. The chatter is often ruminating over past events or concerning itself with the future, worrying about this or that, rehearsing or revising conversations, and much more. As a martyr, your thoughts are a catalyst for negative self-perpetuating cycles.

Experts estimate an average person thinks tens of thousands of thoughts a day. If you notice and pay attention to these thoughts, you will discover that most of them are pointless, useless, and unimportant. You will find that many of these thoughts are negative and repetitive. Earlier in this book, we referred to negative thoughts stick like Velcro, and positive thoughts stick like Teflon. In Cognitive Behavioral Terms, known as CBT, term these thoughts as ANTs (Automatic Negative Thoughts).

It is your conscious mind that chatters incessantly at a superficial level, sometimes called the 'monkey mind.' The conscious mind is also referred to as the tip of the iceberg – the part that you can see above water. Whereas the deeper subconscious and unconscious mind remain out of your awareness, submerged into the stillness of the deep sea. It is here in the unconscious where the deeper layer is ever-present.

Whether your preference is hypnosis or meditation, both aim to focus you on the here and now. It trains your mind to become still. Here you experience tranquillity or the 'sweet spot', the space of high suggestibility that hypnosis and mediation aim for.

Chapter 17

Read-Aloud Smartyr Self-Hypnosis

You have progressed far in this book, which means you are ready to reprogram your smartyr mind and fully embed positive messages and leave the life of the martyr behind. The series of six smartyr self-hypnosis is designed with genuine care and love that targets a specific area related to particular chapters in this book. Using our read–aloud smartyr self-hypnosis, as suggested, will automatically change your mind to think in smartyr terms.

As you have already read, you will continue to realize that your mind is the manifestation of all thought, perception, determination, memory, emotion, and imagination that takes place within your mind. In the following sections, we would like to explain the effectiveness of smartyr self-hypnosis and the best way to do them. If you want your get your positive thoughts to stick like Velcro, all this is possible.

Having qualified in hypnosis for psychotherapy, we have experienced the incredible effects of hypnosis and mediation on all aspects of life. We, too, have personally benefited from the kind of help from the smartyr self-hypnosis like the ones we provide in this book.

We provide you with real guidance to get practicing and utilizing your mind as a powerful tool. Please note that hypnosis and self-hypnosis are deeply personal experiences. You will learn it in your own unique and individual way. The practice of hypnosis will not heal or change anything in your life if you do not expect things to change or have the belief it works.

We have designed this self-hypnosis series to be read aloud with beneficial suggestions to be a complete form of hypnotic therapy from beginning to end. We recommend the minimum requirement to complete the series is to read one smartyr script each day in the same sequence for six weeks. Each hypnosis has a purposeful repetitive opening, relaxation, and ending because familiarity at getting started adds to the powerful trance-like state needed in hypnosis. This method works more powerfully when used regularly and with commitment.

You do not need to have any prior knowledge of hypnotic protocols or be a hypnosis specialist, nor is there any pressure to memorize anything. There is minimal need for preparation to get you started because we have provided you with everything.

The six read-aloud smartyr self-hypnosis series is designed to challenge your martyr mind and cultivate your smartyr mind. To become smartyr not a martyr, we have incorporated both elements of self-hypnosis and meditation. It will induce the process of both an intrinsic shift and external change, primarily focusing on inward attention so that change is experienced as a good feeling.

Our aim is to get you to release your negative thinking through autosuggestion. Connect and rewire your body with your mind, and effectively program positivity into your smartyr mind. While you read-aloud the self-hypnosis scripts, you will drift into a natural auto-pilot mode. Your faculties are bypassed by the Critical Factor, where your subconscious mind can find its sweet spot, allowing it to become malleable for embedding positive outcomes.

With the Critical Factor in suspense, your mind goes into a highly focused state. This helps you become familiar with strengthening and focusing your mind, amplifying your abilities, and becoming mindful and deliberate at what information you allow your subconscious to absorb.

Read–Aloud Smartyr Self-Hypnosis Scripts

Our well–designed scripts are specially worded to engage your brain centers so that that your conscious mind is misdirected as you speak the words and scan the lines on the page. Your autonomic nervous system will be stimulated and become activated. Your senses become open to autosuggestion. Effectively, the subliminal messages are deliberately targeted to bypass your Critical Factor even though your eyes are wide open.

The scripts are formulated to plant new seeds into fertile soil. Changes are made in the subconscious where the fertile soil is and where most of your limiting beliefs and perceptions lie. The emphasis of planting new seeds is to remind you of the positive characteristics that are innate within you, deeply forgotten and disowned.

Remember, you make the change. The smartyr self-hypnosis is simply the starting point, and your deliberate practice is the effective portal to smartyrdom. Focusing your attention requires your full awareness providing an environment for consciousness to be light, clear, and unburdened. Your focused attention and awareness while reading aloud creates the ideal environment for your intuition to be trusted and your imagination to emerge.

Smartyr self-hypnosis is more effective when you are open and willing to learn something new and valuable. Having the right attitude towards practicing the art of self-hypnosis is essential. Hypnosis is a powerful therapeutic tool and a serious practice requiring your time, attention, commitment, and compassionate inquiry.

When you engage in regular practice, the more proficient you will become and the greater depth your practice will be. You will experience the countless benefits for improved mental abilities, emotional states, and physicality. Deep down, you already know how to solve the problems that trouble you, despite any negative thoughts or deeply held beliefs you imagine are holding you back. When in a trance-like state of consciousness, your desire for positive growth leads you to solution-focused attention, and resolutions to your life problems come easily and effortlessly. As you naturally connect deeper into your intuition, you become more visually creative, thus develop profound insight and awareness for your natural Self to emerge.

It has to be stated that the read-aloud smartyr self-hypnosis suggested is not a form of clinical treatment for medical or psychological problems. If you have any psychological or medical condition that you think might be exacerbated by the smartyr self-hypnosis provided in this book, cease practice immediately. We recommend that you seek qualified advice.

Chapter 18

Preparing for Smartyr Self-Hypnosis

We recommend the minimum requirement to complete the series is to read one smartyr script each day in the same sequence for six weeks. For example, Monday: I Am. Tuesday: Connect thoughts with feelings. Wednesday: Awakening your smartyr Self. Thursday: Intrinsic motivation. Friday: Cultivate empathy and compassion. Saturday: Developing your character and charisma.

When you are induced into a relaxed and hypnotic state while reading, you may not necessarily feel hypnotized. Light levels of trance can barely be noticed. Still, as you moderate your voice to the appropriate need for relaxation, its effect is deeper and more therapeutic than you experience.

Read–aloud smartyr self–hypnosis is more effective when you combine your voice with conscious visual scanning of the page. It targets the contents to predictably produce a self–hypnotic state in which you can naturally, and without effort, absorb the therapeutic autosuggestions directly into your subconscious mind.

You will not be consciously aware of how this phenomenon occurs. Nor will you be interested to know because your voice is used to maintain focus on your chosen subject. You will place particular emphasis on instructions for your smartyr mind to absorb effortlessly.

As you settle and prepare yourself to read-aloud, expand your awareness to your physical sensations, and begin to observe your breath. As breathing is part of our autonomic system, we tend to ignore and take it for granted as it happens so naturally. It remains an unconscious act until we focus mindfully on it. Your breath is the very life force that nourishes your every moment, and with practice, you will become at one with it.

Taking a conscious breath brings you to the very epicenter of the present moment. This powerful centering element of breathing and engaging the breath brings awareness into focus creating space for your thoughts and allows the subconscious to get ready for reprogramming.

You will allow self-hypnosis to occur naturally and spontaneously, so relax, expect nothing. You do not need to force your practice to be a certain way. When you use self-hypnosis regularly, the impact of your reading intensifies, and feelings may stir while reading elements of the scripts. This indicates that you are reaching a deeper level of hypnosis and that your skill is improving, and change is happening.

Distractions

It is important to know that our read-aloud smartyr self-hypnosis is about centering your mind for exploration and clarity. Understandably, it is normal to find your mind going off track with internal or external distractions, even while reading out loud. If you catch yourself worrying or having thoughts that distract you, gently remind yourself that these are just thoughts. Patiently bring your attention and focus back to your reading.

While focusing on the words you read, you may encounter a range of other disturbances causing disruption. In general, awareness sounds like a barking dog, a car alarm, children playing, or the gurgling of your belly are regular everyday occurrences but can be experienced as a nuisance.

Whether you experience your own bodily sounds or become disrupted by some external noise, we encourage you to use any disagreeable sound to your mindful advantage. So, rather than become distracted by them, allow them to become a watchful part of the background. Just let them go, just allow them to be, make them part of your moment; no need to change anything or react to it. Just incorporate them into the autosuggestions during your practice. However, be assured you will automatically and immediately emerge out of your hypnotic trance and be fully awake and alert. You will be able to attend to any emergency that may require your attention.

Setting Intentions

While reading aloud, you will have the firm belief that self-hypnosis works along with the expectation that you will succeed. This belief helps set your intention to make your read-aloud smartyr self-hypnosis more effective. It will bring you improved self-control, clearer and more empowered behavioral choices. Assertive decision-making by having learned to trust your inner judgment, boosting your positive opinion of yourself, and strengthen your self-worth.

When preparing yourself for the series of six read-aloud smartyr self-hypnosis, remind yourself why you are doing it. You want to have a clear path so you can appraise who you are and who you want to be. You want to enquire and understand the true nature of how you experience your world.

You want to prepare your mind to be present and to free itself from any distortion. This is how you set the right intention. You have been reading this book to become smartyr, not a martyr, so remind yourself that intention is the bedrock to achieve any goal.

Setting these intentions will free you to see and feel what arises during your practice, no matter how wonderful, difficult, or complex. When your body and mind are in a ready state, you will see and experience the intercommunication and relationship between your thoughts, emotions, and responses. This will allow you to awaken and become smartyr.

Effective Use of Your Imagination

Our smartyr self-hypnosis series requires you to have a direct and immediate perception of the workings of your inner and outer reality. You come to understand that effectively, they are one of the same things. Whether you are conscious of it or not, your mind and what it imagines continuously manifests your reality. This is a continuous process.

Imagination is about forming experiences in your mind, which can be re-creations of past experiences or novel and new ideas. Imagination is the ability to form mental images and think about possibilities. We want to emphasize the importance of including your imagination and involving and forming an emotional visual element when engaging in the read–aloud smartyr self–hypnosis.

Picturing images are equally effective, as are the words that are being embedded. You not only need to hear the words, but you also need to include a 'positive felt–sense feeling' in your body while you also visualize what it 'looks like' for you. This is how you manifest all your creations.

For example, when you have a cup of tea, you have already manifested it using your imagination. But you think you made a conscious intention; however, your legs do not make their way to the kettle by themselves. Your mind had to tell your legs to move. It takes a whole series of automatic routines and actions that go to make up each step. You would have had to visualize or imagine a cup of tea before you consciously chose and desired it. You could say that you deliberately intended on a cup of tea. Still, effectively, your subconscious mind had already lined it up for it to happen.

Manifesting a cup of tea is easy because it is a re-creation of a past experience; you already know how to make it, so it an automatic series of events created from the impressions made upon your mind. Now, imagine the same process happening in your mind for new experiences and more significant changes. Now take a moment and really think about what we have just said.

Your mind has already lined up its outer reality based on the impressions from your unconscious. Your mind does not care what you focus on as your world reflects back to you the evidence of your reality as either a smartyr or a martyr; the mind does not discriminate. Even a cup of tea can be received as either a good or bad experience; it is up to you!

Therefore, when practicing our read-aloud smartyr self-hypnosis, it is helpful to know that the unconscious does not know the difference between reality and fantasy. It cannot differentiate between negative or positive input.

It is skilful imagination and picturing yourself as the smartyr you want to be that actively mixes up the brain creating the gateway to change deeply ingrained habitual negative thinking and patterns of behavior into new ways of thinking and being.

For example, when reading the smartyr self-hypnosis on Developing Your Character and Charisma, in chapter 24, Developing Smartyr Social Skills, imagine yourself as the smartyr thriving in social settings. Imagine yourself getting along with people easily and enjoying the interaction. Visualize what it feels like to be popular and imagine making small talk and keeping a conversation going. Envisage relaxing with friends and what it feels like. Picture your infectious energy and your own sense of fun and spontaneity.

When reading out loud the smartyr self-hypnosis, *be* the smartyr, imagine from it, rather than of it. Imagine yourself gifted with the personality traits of being socially receptive and responsive. Imagine how easy and effective it feels in your body to be with others in this present moment as if it is happening now.

If you have difficulty imagining what it feels like or looks like, finds a person you can see these qualities in, either in real life or within a fictional character. Imagine stepping into the persona of the socially adept smartyr that you wish to emulate.

Focus on all their qualities from all the different perspectives; what they say, how they say it, what they do, how they carry themselves, the energy they exude, etc. Be them from their perspective, copy their skills and feel these qualities as if they are yours. Essentially, link your mind with your body; feel it as if it is happening now. This is the practice of imagination.

You may feel concerned that you cannot picture vivid images in your mind when encouraged to do so. What is more important is to feel the emotion while reading the script and leaving the visualization part to your unconscious mind as that part of your mind will automatically do it for you. The more you practice, vivid visualization will become more accessible and more evident for you.

These mental impressions will give rise to the pictures you seek. Naturally, your mind cannot help but visualize and imagine images written in the script. It is an automatic and unconscious process. The more you engage in this high-powered combination and impress these images onto the subconscious mind, the more persuasive and powerful the read-aloud smartyr self-hypnosis will be. When you embody the positive emotions along with an active visualization, you will fast-track your progress to becoming your social smartyr Self.

Remember, you cannot be induced into hypnosis without your desire or permission. You cannot be convinced to become anything that is not in keeping with your principles and moral code. Fear not, with your consent and firm intention, brain wave vibrations are allowed to slow down through active concentration, enabling you to access a pleasant state of relaxation and into an absorbed focus of attention.

However, it is rare to experience problematic effects from self-hypnosis. We advise that if you experience sudden anxiety or are struggling with anxiety before you begin, you should postpone self-hypnotic practice and, again, seek medical advice.

Getting Settled – Environment

Before you start, settle yourself by creating a comfortable environment. This will help set your intention to engage in the read–aloud smartyr self-hypnosis. Find a place where you will be comfortable, and make sure you set time aside to partake from start to finish. It is better to avoid being under time constraints. This can interfere with you relaxing fully and engaging in your self-hypnosis. So, decide if the hypnosis script you wish to read is conducive to how much time is available to you.

Silence phones, gadgets, and notifications, or turn them off entirely for the duration while you read. Consider family members, pets, or home deliveries from needing your attention.

Consider if you would like to light a candle or burn some incense. Creating a space with a pleasant scent or atmospheric lighting can be comforting. You might want to play some music in the background. Music is a very personal choice, so make sure it is complimentary to induce your hypnotic state, so it does not disrupt you reading out loud. We highly recommend having a metronome ticking in the background to set the pace, as it can help deepen your relaxation. You can download a metronome app on your phone, and you can experiment with the range of pace. We suggest 50 beats per minute but experiment with what works for you.

Make yourself physically as comfortable as possible as you want to avoid having to fidget while reading. We suggest a neutral position is advisable to avoid distractions caused by any likely discomfort. If you find you are drawn to cross your arms or legs, it may be an indicator of stress, and hypnosis is less likely to be effective. Therefore, the most important aspect is to become as relaxed as possible and assume a comfortable position with a neutral posture allowing you to stay grounded and focused.

Choose a suitable chair that is not too comfortable that causes you to slump or doze off. A chair that is reasonably upright is a good option. However, if you are a practiced yogi, then you can sit according to your preference. If you find it preferable to read in bed, you may find it requires more focus to stay awake. You may find sitting at a table is comfortable and relaxing for you.

Regardless of how you position yourself, just find the sweet spot where there is enough tension that your body feels balanced and comfortable. With a focused breath, relax your shoulders, and bring them down, doing whatever feels natural.

Preparing to Read the Smartyr Self-Hypnosis

* Set time aside each day to partake from start to finish and let others know you need at least 20 minutes of privacy.
* Make sure you silence phones, gadgets, and notifications.
* Set the right atmosphere, tone down the lighting but have enough light to read.
* Consider if you want to light a candle or burn some incense.

* Consider playing some complimentary music in the background. Wearing headphones will add a different quality.

* Use a metronome, as we highly recommended it. (You can easily download an app on your phone). Set the pace at 50 beats, but experiment with what works for you.

* Find a place where you will be undisturbed and choose where you want to sit.

* Get physically comfortable and find the sweet spot where your body feels balanced and relaxed.

* Take a focused breath, relax your shoulders, and bring them down, doing whatever feels natural to refine your balance.

* Read the following chapters to prepare you for reading the smartyr self-hypnosis out loud.

Post-Hypnosis Reflections

Pay attention and actively observe the subtle differences before and after your reading. Do not judge outcomes in terms of searching for immediate positive change, but rather, focus your attention on the subtle differences between before and after each self-hypnotic session.

Your results will vary depending on your regularity and repetition of completing the series. We advise that you notice, observe, and feel into the subtle shifts in your daily interactions. This is the trajectory for preferable life changes to eventually occur.

If you experience the emergence of persistent and difficult feelings, you may find it helpful to work through them in a relational setting. You can use this book and its practices alongside entering professional counseling as a companion guide. You may need to work through deeply buried and defended emotional wounds to raise awareness around them; it will significantly benefit your practice.

Thankfully, to become smartyr is about allowing light to shine on any unresolved emotional wounds. If you encounter a recurring theme during the read–aloud smartyr self-hypnosis, especially the kind that causes emotional pain or discomfort, nourish it in awareness, breathe with it, embrace it, and give yourself compassion, explore it further. This kind of clearing of the subconscious is one of the most powerful ways that smartyr self-hypnosis will help you reach your highest and best Self.

Become Smartyr not a Martyr

'I Am' – The Two Most Powerful Words

Chapter 19

Become Smartyr not a Martyr

We now move on to help you find ways to develop your smartyr Self.

Remember, slow down your journey through this book. Realize that your inner Self is doing the best it can right now. You must first think in terms of being a smartyr before you manifest becoming a smartyr. Whatever your feelings are, think about how you feel and begin making friends with them; accept them as yours, however painful or difficult they may feel. Giving yourself a hard time is not conducive to becoming a smartyr. Once you have accepted and owned your feelings, listen to what they are trying to tell you. If they do not go away, then the feeling is trying to tell you something because you have not listened to the message yet. Ask yourself, 'what is this feeling trying to tell me?'

Also, pay attention to what your body is telling you. Your body stores every memory and every interaction you have ever had. When you pay attention to your body, the emotion will give you a physical sensation. Where is the sensation in your body? How intense is it? Is it constant, or does it change? This kind of inquiry, even doing this for just a few minutes, may help you to feel differently and help you identify some important observations about yourself.

Other people, especially your friends and loved ones, may see aspects you cannot see for yourself. Practice seeing yourself as a friend might see you. Imagine you are like them and take on some of their characteristics; stand like them, be like them, breathe like them and notice how you look through their eyes and how they might feel about you. You can gain much from seeing yourself from the outside or pulling the camera back and watching the scene like a movie. When you adopt and practice these exercises, you are honing and cultivating empathy and self-compassion.

If you have strong emotions about something, it can motivate you to behave in a certain way and express specific feelings. For instance, if anger informs you about injustice, it could activate you to right the wrong. You would then have used your emotion to serve you well. Suppose it causes you to lash out with damaging insults or with physical harm; anger becomes a disservice and could present a problem for you. You are much more likely to get emotionally hijacked when you do not know what is happening.

Recognizing the onset of any intense emotion before it causes harm to you or others places you on the front foot to respond effectively. To be angry with the right person at the right time to the right degree and for the right reason takes practice! So be gentle with yourself as you develop into a smartyr.

Feelings can become muddled, and that is because you have opinions about your feelings. For instance, if you feel angry, you might start to feel guilty about that. Keeping an emotional journal can be helpful. Write daily at the end of each day. You will be surprised how much you learn about yourself if you free-flow your writing without censoring or judging yourself.

When your feelings become too complicated, you can sometimes deny your unpleasant feelings and instead push them out, onto, and into other people. This phenomenon is known as Projection. Psychological projection is a defense mechanism. It is employed when you unconsciously attribute your disowned feelings, desires, and ideas to others, distorting the way you see them.

For example, suppose you find that you are often complaining and blaming others. In that case, it is more insight-directed if you ask, 'have I disowned that attribute in me and now see it in the other person?'. For instance, if the statement is, 'you don't listen, ask yourself, is there an attribute in me that is not listening?' Or another self-inquiry is to ask, 'What angers me? Am I angry?'

Moreover, I can also be like them or that person. This self-inquiry helps you learn to stop basing your relationships on assumptions and making people become carriers of your own perceived flaws and ideas. Martyrs believe everyone else is responsible for their misery.

Do not judge yourself for having feelings and experiencing them because they do not indicate your true essence. Feelings change like the weather; they come and go, and they vary from day-to-day. Our read-aloud smartyr self-hypnosis is a useful method of becoming aware, identifying them, and settling into your feelings. The busyness and distractions of everyday life can be pretty confusing. Often, creative ideas come when you take yourself to a quiet place, particularly if you use some of that time to follow the hypnotic meditations in this book.

An excellent place to start is to listen to your heart because the heart is the source of love and acceptance in relation to Self and others. Listening to your heart helps you understand your feelings when problems cannot be solved by logic. Practice by closing your eyes and breathe into the heart area. Notice the emergence of new insights or intuitive feelings or what is happening in your gut or other bodily sensations. When we view matters from our heart and gut, our feelings and perspective about life can change.

Once you commit to self-development, you will be surprised how old behavioral patterns of acting out can be transformed into living authentically. Sharing what you feel with at least one safe person, such as a counselor or psychotherapist, will help clarify negative thinking and the compulsion to repeat unhealthy behavior patterns.

A professional therapist provides a space for you to experience a non-judgmental, non-defensive, empathic, and compassionate dialog, unlike friends and family who can flounder and become entangled in yet another triangle of drama with you. Daring to have a non-abusive relationship with a therapist will cut right through the misery of martyrdom and where you can freely express precisely how you feel and think. Honest dialog with no hidden agenda may feel disorientating at first. You are allowing yourself to change your old habits by being empathically challenged to view and explore your life from a smartyr perspective.

I AM

✴

Smartyr
Self-hypnosis

How to Read the Smartyr Script Out Loud

* We recommend the minimum requirement to complete the series is to read one smartyr script each day in the same sequence for six weeks. This method works more powerfully when used regularly and with commitment

* Before you start, check-in with how you feel using the following list. Mentally scan your body and tick the boxes that best describe how you feel

* Read the script right through from start to finish, it is important you take your time because each hypnosis is purposefully repetitive which adds to the powerful relaxation and trance-like state which is needed for hypnosis

* Start reading aloud in a slow, calm, and purposeful assertive tone

* Pronounce each word fully so it feels like the message you want to convey

* Pause and take a breath where indicated by the dots within the script

* If using a metronome, set it at 50, and allow two full beats before continuing to read

* Read-aloud words written in bold, extended, and italics with emphasis and conviction

* When you finish, check-out with how you feel. Mentally scan your body and tick the boxes that best describe how you feel, compare with your check-in

* Use the journaling pages at the end of each hypnosis to support your progress, insights, thoughts, and reflections

Pre Self-hypnosis
Check-in

Negative	Despair	Angry	Insignificant
Resentful	Low	Frustrated	Suspicious
Critical	Guilty	Disapproving	Miserable
Neutral	Confused	Inquisitive	Vulnerable
Relieved	Excited	Amazed	Interested
Furious	Hopeless	Disappointed	Powerful
Stuck	Determined	Trapped	Blocked
Bitter	Unhappy	Impressed	Disgruntled
Alive	Let Down	Irritated	Anxious
Joyful	Nervous	Annoyed	Insecure
Resistant	Hesitant	Happy	Weak
Bored	Cautious	Powerless	Rejected
Content	Hopeful	Grief	Embarrassed
Curious	Inspired	Victimised	Fearful
Awful	Neglected	Optimistic	Surprised
Scared	Overwhelmed	Lonely	Creative
Inadequate	Helpless	Energetic	Heartbroken
Tense	Calm	Tired	Hesitant
Eager	Worried	Hurt	Safe
Restless	Apprehensive	Regretful	Grateful
Unsure	Judgemental	Confident	Valued
Shocked	Worthless	Thankful	Abandoned
Playful	Glad	Depressed	Withdrawn

I Am
Smartyr Self-Hypnosis

every time I read the **words in bold..** and with every suggestion I give myself, **will** sink in **so deeply** into the unconscious part of my mind, **now**.. feeling settled and taking in a deep breath.... I continue to focus on my breath.. I allow my body to become more settled and more relaxed.. I feel a tingling on the top of my head.. as I continue to become more and more relaxed.. I feel gently at peace.. fully at ease.. totally safe.. and perfectly secure and comfortable..

as my relaxation **deepens, now**.. I feel a wonderful sense of calmness traveling down the back of my head.. I have a sense of warmth and sense of tingling and I have become **more** and **more relaxed**.. I welcome this gentle and warm relaxation filling my body, **now**..

as I read out loud.. I can feel this sense of relaxation moving the down the front of my face.. and I feel the tiny muscles around my eyes relaxing.. my mouth relaxing.. and my jaw relaxing.. to the soothing and calming tone of my voice..

my breath is in tune with my heartbeat, making me feel a **deeper** sense of **relaxation**.. this wonderful sense of **calm**.. and peace moves down my neck and relaxes my shoulders and my chest.. as I continue to read out loud the soothing sound of my voice relaxes the rest of my body.. right to the soles of my feet.. tingling and becoming perfectly **relaxed**.. as I continue to focus on my breath.... becoming more and more **relaxed**..

every time I read the **words in bold..** and with every suggestion I give myself, **will** sink in **so deeply** into the unconscious part of

my mind, *now*.. I see myself moving toward a wide set of well-lit stairs.. I approach this beautiful staircase.. and I am curious where it leads me.. I am surrounded by large protective panes of glass.. and I can clearly see the view.. I feel safe.. as I think about moving *up* these well-lit stairs.. I feel warm as I think about climbing *up* this stunning staircase..

as I take in the view.. I have a sense of anticipation.. as I am looking forward to moving further *up* the staircase.. I feel totally safe, perfectly secure.. as I continue to climb *up* the steps.. I momentarily pause.. taking in a *deep* breath.... I look out of the window and I see the rooftops.. they look like dolls houses.. they are fun and interesting from this view..

from this moment.. as I continue to climb *up*.. I decide to count from one to five... when I reach *five*.. I know I will be perfectly relaxed, and in my own natural state of peace and perfect relaxation.. counting *up now*..

every time I read the *words in bold*.. and with every suggestion I give myself, *will* sink in *so deeply* into the unconscious part of my mind, *now*..

One.. feeling good.. feeling fine.. gently at peace.. fully at ease.. totally safe and perfectly secure.. as I continue to focus on my breath.... I feel myself surrendering to the deep and perfect relaxation that is filling my body.. *now*..

I feel *fine*.. totally safe and perfectly secure.. moving *up*.. and yet going into a *deeper* sense of *relaxation*.. every time I say a number out loud.. it causes me to go *deeper* and *deeper* into *relaxation*..

Two.. as I continue to move *up* the stairs, I pause to look out of the window again.. taking in a *deep* breath.... *now*, I see and view the tops of the trees.. they look magnificent..

from this moment, as I continue to climb *up*.. I become more and more curious.. I feel myself becoming *more* and *more* *relaxed*.. gently at peace.. feeling good.. totally safe.. perfectly secure.. moving *up*, yet, going into a *deeper* sense of *relaxation*.. every time I say a number out loud.. it causes me to go deeper and deeper into *relaxation*..

Three.. feeling good, feeling fine.. totally safe.. perfectly secure.. as I continue to focus on my breath.... *now*, I feel myself surrendering to the deep and perfect relaxation that is filling my body.. I feel fine.. totally safe, perfectly secure.. moving *up* the stairs, yet going into a *deeper* sense of *relaxation*.. as I continue to read out loud.. every time I say a number.. it causes me to go even more deeper and *deeper* into **relaxation**.. feeling gently at peace, feeling good.. feeling fine, totally safe.. and perfectly secure..

Four.. feeling good, feeling fine.. and gently at peace.. fully at *ease*.. totally safe and perfectly secure.. as I continue to *breathe deeply*.... I feel myself surrendering to the deep and perfect relaxation, *now*.. filling my body..

as I continue to move *up* the stairs.. I pause to look out of the window again.. taking in a *deep* breath.... I am *now* in awe of the mountain peaks.. I see them glistening from the rays of the sun coming through the clouds.. they look majestic.. and they look glorious..

from this moment.. as I continue to climb *up*.. I become more and more curious as to where this is taking me.. and feel myself *more* and *more relaxed*.. gently at peace.. feeling good.. totally safe.. perfectly secure.. moving *up*, yet going into a deeper sense of relaxation.. every time I say a number out loud.. it causes me to go *deeper* and *deeper* into *relaxation*..

Five.. feeling wonder-struck and totally safe.. perfectly secure.. I take a *deep* breath…. as I have surrendered *now* to the deep and perfect *relaxation* that has *now* filled my body.. I feel fine.. totally safe and perfectly secure..

I reach the top of the staircase.. and see a warden guarding a beautiful archway.. the warden gives me a protective nod.. and I realize that it is *me* who is architect of this stunning staircase.. and it is *me* who has stationed the warden here .. for my protection..

feeling safe and perfectly secure.. I *easily* bypass the warden.. I *easily* walk out onto the balcony.. and find myself gently being in the most comfortable position.. feeling a perfect state of *relaxation*.

as I relax and focus on my breath…. I *now* find myself sitting above the clouds.. I feel completely at *ease* and I begin to feel a *beautiful sensation* of peace and relaxation, tranquility and calm.. I imagine the *ideal me* projected onto the sky like a movie screen *now*.. as I picture myself, my mind and body feels a wonderful *sense of calm*, and feels gently at peace..

I made a *good decision* to climb the staircase, as I can *now* see myself more clearly, and with a better view.. I see myself as I am.. *I Am so relaxed*.. that my mind has become so sensitive..

so receptive to what I read out loud.. that every time I read the *words in bold*.. and with every suggestion I give myself, *will* sink in *so deeply* into the unconscious part of my mind.. that it will begin to cause such a *lasting impression* there, *now*..

tranquility and calm are flowing through my mind and body like a cool breeze, giving me such a pleasant feeling.. such a beautiful sensation... as I embed positive suggestions into my unconscious mind, I *now* acknowledge *my true value*.. these suggestions exercise a greater and *greater influence* to the way I think.. over the way I feel.. over the way I behave.. and the way *I become smartyr*.

every time I read the *words in bold*.. and with every suggestion *I give myself,* will sink in so deeply.. into the unconscious part of my mind.. that it will begin to cause such a *lasting impression, now*.. and *will* remain firmly embedded in the unconscious part of my mind, *now*.. even after I have stopped reading out loud..

I feel good that *I am* interested in improving my life.. and.. just *now*.. *I am* finding ways to develop my smartyr Self.. I can listen to my heart as a source of *love and acceptance* in relation to myself and others..

now.. drifting deeper and deeper all the time as I continue to listen to my voice.. I *hear my voice*, I slow down, I drift deeper and deeper.. I feel a wonderful sense of calm..

now.. I focus into my heart area.. I notice the emergence of *new insights* and *intuitive feelings*, just *now*.. *I am*... fully intuitive and, *in tune with myself*. I realize, my inner self is doing its very best at this time, *now*..

I am good at thinking about my feelings.. and, *I am good* at feeling about my thinking, my heart is a *source of acceptance*.. *I am compassionate* toward myself.. and, *I am clear* with knowing what my feelings are telling me.. and, *I am, good* at paying attention to what my body is telling me..

I am my own best friend.. I see, *I am empathic* towards myself.. and trusting of myself.. *I trust*, I am surrounded.. *I am supported*.. and, *I am encouraged*.. and, *I am committed* to living an *authentic life, now*. . drifting deeper and deeper all the time as I continue to listen to my voice.. my unconscious mind will not eradicate these positive suggestions.. they will help me with my thinking. I will begin to *think more clearly.. more objectively.. more realistically.. more positively, now.*

now.. my suggestions will also help me with my feelings because, *I am courageous*.. and, *I am determined* to succeed becoming *smartyr*.. my courage and determination will also help me with my actions.. and, my behaviors because I pay particular attention to *my thoughts.. my ideas*.. and *my insights* as they give me information about the next steps I need to take.. everything I say will happen for *my own good*.. will happen more and more..

these suggestions will continue to influence and become part of my natural inner dialogue as I go about my day.. every day I will become so deeply interested in whatever *I am doing*.. whatever *I am feeling*.. whatever *I am thinking*.. and whatever is going on around me.. that my mind will be in a state of relaxation..

I am.. going to *feel physically stronger* and.. I will *feel more alert*.. more wide awake.. *more energetic*.. and much less easily discouraged..

I will wake up from my self-hypnotic trance by counting to three.. while reading out-loud.. when I get to number *three*.. I will be wide awake, fully alert, and will be *feeling better than ever before*..

Three.. feeling *satisfied* and *proud*, I am beginning to awaken from my hypnotic trance..

Two. becoming aware of my body, *I am excited* about the positive results from this session..

ONE, ONE, ONE, now, wide awake, refreshed and *feeling better than ever before!*

Post Hypnosis Reflections

* Check-out with how you feel using the following list. Mentally scan your body and tick the boxes that best describe how you feel
* Your results will vary depending on your regularity and repetition on completing the series
* Journal any thoughts, feelings or insights that may emerge on the following pages
* Notice, observe and feel into the subtle shifts in your daily interactions as this is the trajectory for preferable life changes to eventually occur

Post Self-hypnosis
Check-out

Negative		Despair		Angry		Insignificant	
Resentful		Low		Frustrated		Suspicious	
Critical		Guilty		Disapproving		Miserable	
Neutral		Confused		Inquisitive		Vulnerable	
Relieved		Excited		Amazed		Interested	
Furious		Hopeless		Disappointed		Powerful	
Stuck		Determined		Trapped		Blocked	
Bitter		Unhappy		Impressed		Disgruntled	
Alive		Let Down		Irritated		Anxious	
Joyful		Nervous		Annoyed		Insecure	
Resistant		Hesitant		Happy		Weak	
Bored		Cautious		Powerless		Rejected	
Content		Hopeful		Grief		Embarrassed	
Curious		Inspired		Victimised		Fearful	
Awful		Neglected		Optimistic		Surprised	
Scared		Overwhelmed		Lonely		Creative	
Inadequate		Helpless		Energetic		Heartbroken	
Tense		Calm		Tired		Hesitant	
Eager		Worried		Hurt		Safe	
Restless		Apprehensive		Regretful		Grateful	
Unsure		Judgemental		Confident		Valued	
Shocked		Worthless		Thankful		Abandoned	
Playful		Glad		Depressed		Withdrawn	

Journaling
Insights - Thoughts - Reflections

Journaling
Insights - Thoughts - Reflections

The Foundation of Emotions and Feelings

Chapter 20

The Foundation of Emotions and Feelings

In neuroscience and psychology, understanding emotions and feelings is a significant area of constant research and growth. All humans experience emotions – they are primary and evolutionary, and hard-wired.

There is much debate on how many primary emotions there are. Different theories debate the four primary emotions of anger, fear, sadness, and joy. In contrast, some suggest there are eight. For this book, we refer to six basic human emotions: happy, anger, sad, fear, surprise, and disgust.

Much of this debate exists because emotions are universal and fit into different cultural contexts. In other words, how you conceptualize, name, and experience your emotions is culturally and environmentally determined. All cultures in the world have their version of primary emotions. Society is becoming more culturally diverse. Psychologists and researchers continue to debate how evolutionary predictions and social evolutionary pressures influence the primary list of emotions. However, our concepts in this book depend on psychology in Western culture and the English language.

You may wonder how to differentiate between being in touch with emotions and experiencing feelings. Despite the confusion which comes first, neuroscientific research has found that our emotions are aroused before our feelings are triggered. A new-born baby is a bundle of emotions, pure and simple. Feelings associated with raw emotions in the infant cannot be differentiated until they develop enough cognition to rationalize, control, recognize and express their feelings.

Emotions and feelings are often used interchangeably and defining them is often tricky. We know that your emotions are experienced through your physical body, and your feelings are a self-expression of your emotions that your body is experiencing. Emotions are evolutionary and hard-wired; therefore, they cannot be learned, but your feelings associated with your emotions are.

For instance, anger is a hard-wired primary emotion. Still, words such as irritation, frustration, and even the feeling of full-blown rage, are all feeling words associated with the emotion of anger. You could literally feel your blood boiling, bite someone's head off or even blow a fuse. Using feeling words can depend on your perception of a situation because feelings are a mental construct. Therefore, you can learn about yourself and others when you think about what is happening in and outside yourself. Your thoughts create your feelings, and your feelings determine your behavior. Primarily, emotions, feelings, and behavior play an essential role in your daily life. There is always a primary unconscious emotion physically rooted that drives your reality. Through the practice of self-awareness, it supports you to gain insight and understanding of what is happening around you, which determines your life as experienced as stressful or calm.

Your instinct is your emotional radar which also unconsciously informs you about how you are feeling. If you are angry, on some level, you must construe something as offensive, and it is through your thinking that you then decide how you feel. Feelings give you a choice on how to behave. Feeling words, such as irritation and frustration, are useful in determining your outward expression of the angry emotional response.

As humans, you cannot choose the primary emotions of happy, anger, sad, fear, surprise, and disgust; they are innate within each of us. Emotions create the physical states in your body, which react automatically to the external stimuli to the world around you. Emotions can be observed through your physical reaction and scientifically measured by blood flow, brain activity, facial expression/tone, and bodily stance. They are carried out by the limbic system (your emotional processing center) in the brain.

On the other hand, feelings are triggered by your thoughts and reactions to your primary emotions and cannot be scientifically measured. This means that feelings are a mental construct from which you make associations acquired through your life experience.

For example, when you experience the emotion of fear from, let's say, a dominating parent, various feelings can emerge, such as dread, panic, anxiety, and anticipation. Your body response is an adrenaline rush, your heart beats faster, you begin to sweat, and your thought process is to decide to fight or flight. Your emotions do not exist in isolation; context is everything.

You experience feelings always in the present, raw, and live despite being a familiar re-enactment of the past. When fear is looming, your feelings associated with this primary emotion will depend on your early experiences, either from the environment or related to your primary caregivers.

For instance, if you grew up in an unpredictable home environment, you are more likely to be hypervigilant, and your feelings of anticipation and readiness will be figural. Your emotions and feelings will go on to play an influential role in how you experience and interact with people and the world. This, in turn, influences the development of your identity and your personal reality. If these feelings are left unexplored, they can prompt a never-ending cycle of panic, pain, and confusion. You can begin to identify yourself into role types such as worriers, depressives, givers, caretakers, or aggressors.

You may not always like what you see. But there is comfort in knowing yourself and the ability to grow and evolve from the identity and role that was initially created when you had limited choice. By becoming self-aware, allows you to self-evaluate in relation to others. At this point, you make your inner world the focus of attention to get to know yourself and navigate your environment. This is different from feelings of self-consciousness, which is more to do with falling into a trap of self-absorption.

It is about knowing who you are when you are not playing your 'roles' in life. It is about your traits, attitudes, core values, and beliefs and how these define your character and identity. These traits impact your behavior and decisions. People and your environment will offer you feedback, given that your behaviors and decisions are the easiest to recognize. This provides you with an opportunity to question what you do and why you do it, and this will allow you to self-reflect and modify yourself if needed.

Self-awareness is rare, even amongst humans. It is the opposite of blissful ignorance. Self-awareness provides you with insight into things you cannot and do not always want to see. It is a complex internal process of self-reflection and having an intra-personal capacity to identify your emotions, feelings, inner thoughts, and bodily sensations. Human beings are complex and diverse. Observing your thoughts and feelings as they occur is a precious attribute. It raises your self-awareness and provides you with a stronger sense of Self.

'What you don't know about yourself CAN hurt you': As a smartyr with emotional self-awareness, you will know when others transfer their opinions, thoughts, beliefs, and ideas onto and into you. You understand your inner landscape, know your own emotions, and recognize what feelings are being attributed to and into you from others. You do not absorb these feelings as if they belong to you. Instead, you can navigate your internal emotions associated with the accompanying feelings, which give you greater control over your life and relationships - a prerequisite to success.

A great deal of your unconscious psychic energy is spent witnessing, processing, and interpreting your emotions in every interaction with others. How you respond to your own sophisticated emotional experience can determine how you choose to express or hide your feelings. Part of your socialization requires you to regulate and, at times, filter your feelings. You can conceal certain feelings and use them as a defense to protect your emotions at any given time. For instance, you can be angry when truly you are feeling sad. You may show happiness when feeling resentful or showing hostility when you prefer to be held and soothed instead.

Just imagine feeling socially anxious, and you must attend an event. You find yourself needing to bolster your anxiety with unnatural extroversion and to portray energetic enthusiasm. This would mean you filter the anxiety and the physical reaction within your body of, say, anger and resentment for having to attend the event you would rather avoid. Your nervous system takes the toll.

This kind of filtering results in negative outcomes and is probably due to having low self-esteem and an inability to knowingly assert yourself. If this is your status quo, emotional burn-out will be inevitable, and you will become a victim of your circumstances. You will eventually adopt the identity of a martyr.

Imagine yourself as J.D., you hear that your friend is going traveling for 6 months. You experience a gut-wrenching physical reaction and feel envy towards your friend's freedom and courage. But you filter and hide your emotional reaction and choose instead to express feelings of delight and excitement so you can share in your friend's joy.

As a smartyr, you can regulate your feelings and accept that your friend is more affluent and freer than you. You can understand your internal feelings of envy, and you might even choose to express these envious feelings towards your friend in a light-hearted tone. With this knowing, insight, and self-awareness, your smartyr Self does not sabotage your valuable friendship by acting out any unconscious negative feelings of resentment and bitterness at the perceived unfairness that your friend has more than you.

Instead, as a smartyr, your awareness of your own envy could lead you to meet your own unmet needs. Knowing your feelings can help you set your own intentions and inspire you to reach your own potential and access your deepest desire. You could, for instance, take a sabbatical and go traveling.

Connect Thoughts with Feelings

✴

Smartyr Self-hypnosis

How to Read the Smartyr Script Out Loud

* We recommend the minimum requirement to complete the series is to read one smartyr script each day in the same sequence for six weeks. This method works more powerfully when used regularly and with commitment

* Before you start, check-in with how you feel using the following list. Mentally scan your body and tick the boxes that best describe how you feel

* Read the script right through from start to finish, it is important you take your time because each hypnosis is purposefully repetitive which adds to the powerful relaxation and trance-like state which is needed for hypnosis

* Start reading aloud in a slow, calm, and purposeful assertive tone

* Pronounce each word fully so it feels like the message you want to convey

* Pause and take a breath where indicated by the dots within the script

* If using a metronome, set it at 50, and allow two full beats before continuing to read

* Read-aloud words written in bold, extended, and italics with emphasis and conviction

* When you finish, check-out with how you feel. Mentally scan your body and tick the boxes that best describe how you feel, compare with your check-in

* Use the journaling pages at the end of each hypnosis to support your progress, insights, thoughts, and reflections

Pre Self-hypnosis Check-in

Negative	Despair	Angry	Insignificant
Resentful	Low	Frustrated	Suspicious
Critical	Guilty	Disapproving	Miserable
Neutral	Confused	Inquisitive	Vulnerable
Relieved	Excited	Amazed	Interested
Furious	Hopeless	Disappointed	Powerful
Stuck	Determined	Trapped	Blocked
Bitter	Unhappy	Impressed	Disgruntled
Alive	Let Down	Irritated	Anxious
Joyful	Nervous	Annoyed	Insecure
Resistant	Hesitant	Happy	Weak
Bored	Cautious	Powerless	Rejected
Content	Hopeful	Grief	Embarrassed
Curious	Inspired	Victimised	Fearful
Awful	Neglected	Optimistic	Surprised
Scared	Overwhelmed	Lonely	Creative
Inadequate	Helpless	Energetic	Heartbroken
Tense	Calm	Tired	Hesitant
Eager	Worried	Hurt	Safe
Restless	Apprehensive	Regretful	Grateful
Unsure	Judgemental	Confident	Valued
Shocked	Worthless	Thankful	Abandoned
Playful	Glad	Depressed	Withdrawn

Connect Thoughts with Feelings
Smartyr Self-Hypnosis

every time I read the **words in bold..** and with every suggestion I give myself, **will** sink in **so deeply** into the unconscious part of my mind, **now..** feeling settled and taking in a deep breath…. I continue to focus on my breath.. I allow my body to become more settled and more relaxed.. I feel a tingling on the top of my head.. as I continue to become more and more relaxed.. I feel gently at peace.. fully at ease.. totally safe.. and perfectly secure and comfortable..

as my relaxation **deepens, now..** I feel a wonderful sense of calmness traveling down the back of my head.. I have a sense of warmth and sense of tingling and I have become **more** and **more relaxed..** I welcome this gentle and warm relaxation filling my body, **now..**

as I read out loud.. I can feel this sense of relaxation moving the down the front of my face.. and I feel the tiny muscles around my eyes relaxing.. my mouth relaxing.. and my jaw relaxing.. to the soothing and calming tone of my voice..

my breath is in tune with my heartbeat, making me feel a **deeper** sense of **relaxation..** this wonderful sense of **calm..** and peace moves down my neck and relaxes my shoulders and my chest.. as I continue to read out loud the soothing sound of my voice relaxes the rest of my body.. right to the soles of my feet.. tingling and becoming perfectly **relaxed..** as I continue to focus on my breath…. becoming more and more **relaxed..**

every time I read the **words in bold..** and with every suggestion I give myself, **will** sink in **so deeply** into the unconscious part of

139

my mind, *now*.. I see myself moving toward a wide set of well-lit stairs.. I approach this beautiful staircase.. and I am curious where it leads me.. I am surrounded by large protective panes of glass.. and I can clearly see the view.. I feel safe.. as I think about moving *up* these well-lit stairs.. I feel warm as I think about climbing *up* this stunning staircase..

as I take in the view.. I have a sense of anticipation.. as I am looking forward to moving further *up* the staircase.. I feel totally safe, perfectly secure.. as I continue to climb *up* the steps.. I momentarily pause.. taking in a *deep* breath.... I look out of the window and I see the rooftops.. they look like dolls houses.. they are fun and interesting from this view..

from this moment.. as I continue to climb *up*.. I decide to count from one to five... when I reach *five*.. I know I will be perfectly relaxed, and in my own natural state of peace and perfect relaxation.. counting *up now*..

every time I read the *words in bold*.. and with every suggestion I give myself, *will* sink in *so deeply* into the unconscious part of my mind, *now*..

One.. feeling good.. feeling fine.. gently at peace.. fully at ease.. totally safe and perfectly secure.. as I continue to focus on my breath.... I feel myself surrendering to the deep and perfect relaxation that is filling my body.. *now*..

I feel *fine*.. totally safe and perfectly secure.. moving *up*.. and yet going into a *deeper* sense of *relaxation*.. every time I say a number out loud.. it causes me to go *deeper* and *deeper* into *relaxation*..

Two.. as I continue to move *up* the stairs, I pause to look out of the window again.. taking in a *deep* breath.... *now*, I see and view the tops of the trees.. they look magnificent..

from this moment, as I continue to climb *up*.. I become more and more curious.. I feel myself becoming *more* and *more relaxed*.. gently at peace.. feeling good.. totally safe.. perfectly secure.. moving *up*, yet, going into a *deeper* sense of *relaxation*.. every time I say a number out loud.. it causes me to go deeper and deeper into *relaxation*..

Three.. feeling good, feeling fine.. totally safe.. perfectly secure.. as I continue to focus on my breath.... *now*, I feel myself surrendering to the deep and perfect relaxation that is filling my body.. I feel fine.. totally safe, perfectly secure.. moving *up* the stairs, yet going into a *deeper* sense of *relaxation*.. as I continue to read out loud.. every time I say a number.. it causes me to go even more deeper and *deeper* into **relaxation**.. feeling gently at peace, feeling good.. feeling fine, totally safe.. and perfectly secure..

Four.. feeling good, feeling fine.. and gently at peace.. fully at *ease*.. totally safe and perfectly secure.. as I continue to *breathe deeply*.... I feel myself surrendering to the deep and perfect relaxation, *now*.. filling my body..

as I continue to move *up* the stairs.. I pause to look out of the window again.. taking in a *deep* breath.... I am *now* in awe of the mountain peaks.. I see them glistening from the rays of the sun coming through the clouds.. they look majestic.. and they look glorious..

from this moment.. as I continue to climb *up*.. I become more and more curious as to where this is taking me.. and feel myself *more* and *more relaxed*.. gently at peace.. feeling good.. totally safe.. perfectly secure.. moving *up*, yet going into a deeper sense of relaxation.. every time I say a number out loud.. it causes me to go *deeper* and *deeper* into *relaxation*..

Five.. feeling wonder-struck and totally safe.. perfectly secure.. I take a *deep* breath.... as I have surrendered *now* to the deep and perfect *relaxation* that has *now* filled my body.. I feel fine.. totally safe and perfectly secure..

I reach the top of the staircase.. and see a warden guarding a beautiful archway.. the warden gives me a protective nod.. and I realize that it is *me* who is architect of this stunning staircase.. and it is *me* who has stationed the warden here .. for my protection..

feeling safe and perfectly secure.. I *easily* bypass the warden.. I *easily* walk out onto the balcony.. and find myself gently being in the most comfortable position.. feeling a perfect state of *relaxation*.

as I relax and focus on my breath..... I *now* find myself sitting above the clouds.. I feel completely at *ease* and I begin to feel a *beautiful sensation* of peace and relaxation, tranquility and calm.. I imagine the *ideal me* projected onto the sky like a movie screen *now*.. as I picture myself, my mind and body feels a wonderful *sense of calm*, and feels gently at peace..

I made a *good decision* to climb the staircase, as I can *now* see myself more clearly, and with a better view.. I see myself as I am.. *I Am so relaxed*.. that my mind has become so sensitive..

so receptive to what I read out loud.. that every time I read the *words in bold*.. and with every suggestion I give myself, *will* sink in *so deeply* into the unconscious part of my mind.. that it will begin to cause such a *lasting impression* there, *now*..

tranquility and calm are flowing through my mind and body like a cool breeze, giving me such a pleasant feeling.. such a beautiful sensation... as I embed positive suggestions into my unconscious mind, I *now* acknowledge *my true value*.. these suggestions exercise a greater and *greater influence* to the way I think.. over the way I feel.. over the way I behave.. and the way *I become smartyr*.

every time I read the *words in bold*.. and with every suggestion *I give myself,* will sink in so deeply.. into the unconscious part of my mind.. that it will begin to cause such a *lasting impression, now*.. and *will* remain firmly embedded in the unconscious part of my mind, *now*.. even after I have stopped reading out loud..

I feel good that *I am* interested in improving my life.. and.. just *now*.. *I am* finding ways to develop my smartyr Self. I feel good *now*.. I have decided to rewire my mind.. so that my thoughts can synchronize with my feelings.. I can *now* experience a full mind–body connection of who *I truly am*.... I know this is the way forward for me..

now.. drifting deeper and deeper all the time as I continue to listen to my voice.. I *hear my voice*, I slow down, I drift deeper and deeper.. I feel a wonderful sense of calm..

now.. my physical reactions help me *observe my emotions* and.. *now I notice what am feeling*.. what I am feeling helps me understand my thoughts and reactions..

I accept my emotions are experienced through my physical body.. and *I am compassionate* that my feelings are a self-expression of my emotions..

now.. I visualize my inner landscape.. it is *rich and organic* and I recognize my emotions in my body.. and.. *I am skilled* at articulating my emotions as a tangible feeling..

now.. my positive thoughts create my positive feelings, and connecting them to my positive feelings determines *my smartyr behavior*..

my inner world is *now*.. the focus of my attention because *I synchronize my thoughts with my feelings*.. making this connection guides me to navigate my environment.. this supports me to know myself even better.. and *become even more smartyr, now*..

my life is calm and harmonious.. and I trust my instincts as my emotional radar.. these insights intuitively inform me how I feel.. *now*..

I can navigate my emotions .. *I can distinguish* the associated feelings.. this gives me *greater choice* over my life and relationships.. which is a prerequisite to my *success at being smartyr*.. *now*..

connecting my thoughts with my emotions helps me to filter my feelings.. this provides me with positive outcomes.. as *I Am a smartyr living a flourishing life, now*.. I regulate my feelings naturally and authentically.. **I can filter** my feelings consciously.. and from a place of choosing.. *I Am*.. appropriate to the maintenance of all my interpersonal relationships..

I love thinking and feeling in my body who *I have become, now*..

I love thinking and feeling in my body who *I Am, now*..

I love thinking and feeling in my body that, *I Am now, a smartyr*..

these suggestions will continue to influence and become part of my natural inner dialogue as I go about my day.. every day I will become so deeply interested in whatever *I am doing*.. whatever *I am feeling*.. whatever *I am thinking*.. and whatever is going on around me.. that my mind will be in a state of relaxation..

I am.. going to *feel physically stronger* and.. I will *feel more alert*.. more wide awake.. *more energetic*.. and much less easily discouraged..

I will wake up from my self-hypnotic trance by counting to three.. while reading out-loud.. when I get to number *three*.. I will be wide awake, fully alert, and will be *feeling better than ever before*..

Three.. feeling *satisfied* and *proud*, I am beginning to awaken from my hypnotic trance..

Two. becoming aware of my body, *I am excited* about the positive results from this session..

ONE, ONE, ONE, now, wide awake, refreshed and *feeling better than ever before!*

Post Hypnosis Reflections

* Check-out with how you feel using the following list. Mentally scan your body and tick the boxes that best describe how you feel
* Your results will vary depending on your regularity and repetition on completing the series
* Journal any thoughts, feelings or insights that may emerge on the following pages
* Notice, observe and feel into the subtle shifts in your daily interactions as this is the trajectory for preferrable life changes to eventually occur

Post Self-hypnosis
Check-out

Negative	Despair	Angry	Insignificant
Resentful	Low	Frustrated	Suspicious
Critical	Guilty	Disapproving	Miserable
Neutral	Confused	Inquisitive	Vulnerable
Relieved	Excited	Amazed	Interested
Furious	Hopeless	Disappointed	Powerful
Stuck	Determined	Trapped	Blocked
Bitter	Unhappy	Impressed	Disgruntled
Alive	Let Down	Irritated	Anxious
Joyful	Nervous	Annoyed	Insecure
Resistant	Hesitant	Happy	Weak
Bored	Cautious	Powerless	Rejected
Content	Hopeful	Grief	Embarrassed
Curious	Inspired	Victimised	Fearful
Awful	Neglected	Optimistic	Surprised
Scared	Overwhelmed	Lonely	Creative
Inadequate	Helpless	Energetic	Heartbroken
Tense	Calm	Tired	Hesitant
Eager	Worried	Hurt	Safe
Restless	Apprehensive	Regretful	Grateful
Unsure	Judgemental	Confident	Valued
Shocked	Worthless	Thankful	Abandoned
Playful	Glad	Depressed	Withdrawn

Journaling
Insights - Thoughts - Reflections

Journaling
Insights - Thoughts - Reflections

Functions
of your
Internal
Self-Moderator

Chapter 21

Functions of your Internal Self-Moderator

Have you ever said something that you later regretted, or did you manage to stop yourself in time?

Learning to self-moderate is a fundamental function in human life. These are essential aspects to fit within society. Your subjective experience is in direct relation to the on-going demands you encounter that are socially tolerable. Therefore, having the ability to consciously filter your thoughts and feelings provides you with a space in which to assess any consequences from stating things that you instinctively wish to express.

Once you accept that emotions are hardwired and universal, you cannot avoid but feel and experience them mentally and physically. As a smartyr with a developed internal self-moderator, you do not need to second guess what you do or say. Self-moderation is the practice of self-control to avoid responding negatively, which you may regret later. Regulating your thoughts and feelings is a form of filtering that supports the management of your emotional states.

Smartyrs will have cultivated a sense of Self that is aware enough to take personal responsibility for regulating their own subjective experience. These feelings are based on your experience and perception of what is happening. You will have learned how to respond rather than react.

To maintain healthy adult relationships, you need to develop the ability to self-reflect. It supports you to control and manage your emotional states and allows you to set clear boundaries with yourself and others. Taking responsibility for yourself is not easy. It takes conscious awareness and practice to save yourself from any impulsive reactions that you may later regret.

As J.D., imagine you are at work, and you have spent a great deal of time and effort writing a lengthy report to hand in on time. Your work colleague belittles your efforts with suggestions that you could have done a better job.

Your subjective experience is that you believe your colleague is disparaging you on purpose so that you can be told off again because they don't respect you. Your internal persecutor reminds you that you are stupid, or else you would not have been told off.

You truly want to rage and scream at them and throw the computer across the room. Still, because you believe you must work hard and over-stretch yourself to make a difference, you must suppress your feelings.

Unaware that your default position is steeped victimhood, you remain unassertive. You automatically think this situation is hopeless and nothing ever goes right for you, so what's the point of ever trying. Feeling confused, hated, angry, and misjudged, these feelings have triggered a sense of shame and worthlessness.

Feeling overwhelmed, you blush, your heart begins to race, and you feel a cramping pain in your gut. These physical sensations drive you to impulsively storm off and dash to the loo so you can protect and manage the intensity of your overpowering emotions.

The whole experience has triggered doubt in your capabilities. It crushes your sense of worthiness which has sent you into an internal shame attack.

You feel victimized and powerless and wish you had the skills to have handled your feelings with less impulsivity. With more adult functioning, where you could have activated your internal self-moderator, you could have explained yourself with more clarity if only you were smartyr.

Considerations

Imagine that J.D. has decided to become smartyr and not a martyr anymore, and uses the following self-moderating template to help examine and reflect on the situation with the colleague and to make meaning from the experience:

Martyr thoughts:

* Attitudes – Sulking, hostility, defensive, and withdrawal
* Assumptions – What have I done wrong
* Demands – Finish the report on time
* Beliefs – I must work hard and overstretch myself
* Images – Throwing the computer across the room
* Meanings – Nothing ever goes right for me.

Martyr emotions and feelings:

* Physical sensations – overwhelmed, blushing, blood boiling, heart racing, gut ache
* Unhealthy feelings – shame, worthless, persecuted.

Martyr behaviors:

* Destructive behaviors – withdrawal to bathroom, sulking, moody.

When you actively begin to practice writing or mind mapping what emerges using the above checklist, you allow yourself to go into slow motion to assess the situation objectively. This activity also encourages you to build awareness of your thinking, feeling, and behavioral patterns. Over time, you begin to notice links and patterns and become able to separate thoughts from facts.

When a smartyr is caught up in a difficult situation or a challenging moment, they consider the following three statements before responding. These statements help you evaluate self-moderation in any given situation.

* Does it need to be said?
* Does it need to be said by me?
* Does it need to be said by me at this time?

These statements are about you monitoring when the appropriate time or place is to engage with impulsivity and spontaneity. The statements will also help you to evaluate, modify and communicate your interactions and experiences. Engaging with them will allow you to momentarily pause for self-reflection and for you to recognize that there are alternative ways for healthier adult-to-adult interaction.

For example, repeating the exercise so that J.D. can obtain a smartyr outcome. We use the self-moderating template as an example to show renewed reflection for evaluation and development for smartyr practice.

Smartyr thoughts:

* Attitudes – open, objective listening
* Assumptions – clarifies the boundaries
* Demands – deliberate dedication to finish the report on time
* Beliefs – what my colleague thinks about me is ok
* Images – collaboration for clear communication

* Meanings – I have faith that I have delivered a good report.

Smartyr emotions and feelings:

* Physical sensations – calm, composed, open posture
* Healthy feelings – curiosity, worthiness, and satisfaction.

Smartyr behaviors:

* Constructive behaviors – collaborative engagement.

How you choose and what you decide to say and do can only come from within you. Use your thoughts and feelings to inform you so you can choose to shift from a place of powerlessness. For example, 'Why is this always happening to me?' or even worse, perceived powerfulness, 'Why are they making me feel this way?' to one of empowerment, as it allows you to change your situation for a healthier interaction based on clarity and transparency.

Developing self-moderation is a prerequisite for success. For that process to occur, as a smartyr, it is worth developing the skill and ability to moderate your emotional state. Still, it is also imperative that you focus on what is happening in your body. Practice moderating your body's physical sensations to help you when you are in the heat of the moment.

Journaling
Insights - Thoughts - Reflections

Here is the self-moderating template you can use for reflection, evaluation and development for smartyr practice. it is worth developing the skill and ability to moderate your emotional state. When you are caught up in a difficult situation or a challenging moment, consider the following before responding.

These questions help evaluate self-moderation in any given situation
Does it need to be said?
Does it need to be said by me?
Does it need to be said by me at this time?

Smartyr thoughts	
Attitudes	
Assumptions	
Demands	
Beliefs	
Images	
Meanings	
Smartyr emotions and feelings	
Physical sensations	
Healthy feelings	
Smartyr behaviors	
Constructive behaviors	

At first, it may seem pointless and feel awkward to practice. Still, over time as you become familiar with engaging in these exercises, you will become acquainted with your bodily sensations. In time you will begin to value and appreciate the time and effort you give it. You will start to notice a distinctive quality in your interactions with others.

*   **Watch yourself as if you are in a film:** Imagine watching a stressful situation play out on a separate monitor in your mind's eye and reframe the scene
*   **Focus on your breathing:** Check and monitor your body for tension. If there are any tense areas, relax them by imagining that you are breathing into them
*   **Center yourself:** Imagine your feet are firmly rooted to the ground and notice how physically strong and centered you feel. Paying attention to your center will help make you feel stronger and calmer
*   **Stand tall:** Your physical posture can have a significant effect on how you feel. If you are unable to stand, imagine that you can 'grow your bones.' This slight manoeuvre will expand your aura and your energy field
*   **Read out loud** the smartyr self-hypnosis scripts that come with this book to help you reinforce and imbed the positive messages.

Here are some other activities worth practicing so you are more prepared for when things become challenging:

Expand your vision: To expand your peripheral vision, practice the Shaman's 'eagle eye' exercise.

*   Bring your hands in front of your face and wiggle your fingers while looking straight ahead. Move your hands

away from your face and towards your ears, keeping your eyes focused on your wiggling fingers - and broaden your field of vision

* Focus your awareness to include the ceiling and the floor
* Extend your focus even further out, beyond the edges of your vision, and all the way behind you to 360 degrees
* Notice when you come back how calm you feel and how your breathing has slowed down.

This instantly activates the body's relaxation response and works well for both anger and fear.

Anchor your good feelings:

* Recall a memory when you felt calm and relaxed and good about yourself
* Re-live the memory and when the good feelings arise, see the image, make the gesture, or say the word
* Create a visual image, physical gesture, or choose a word that sum up those feelings
* Practice getting into these good feelings until they become embedded. You can then access them anytime you need them, just by recalling the image, gesture, or word.

This will remind you that you have experienced a meaningful moment, and you can experience it again.

Deal with your negative internal voice. This mental chatter lives rent-free in your mind. It keeps a constant negative view of your life and contributes to keeping your self-esteem low.

Negative self-talk is universal and sticks to us like Velcro and positive self-talk sticks to us like Teflon – unless, of course, you are a well-rehearsed smartyr, it will have the opposite effect.

* Notice what your inner chatter is saying
* Hold a pen in the hand you usually write with and write what the negative chatter is saying
* Now, with the other hand, take the pen and respond. Do not censor the chatter. It is the feeling response that is important
* You are creating a dialog between your internal negative chatter and the neglected and disowned parts of yourself. Utilizing the left and right sides of your brain is a way of dialoguing that gives insight and a voice to your feelings and how you have been mistreating and rejecting yourself
* This is an opportunity to really challenge the negative internal self-talk and thinking process
* Observe when you say things like – 'I can't do that,' 'I mustn't, 'I shouldn't' or 'I have to'
* Ask yourself these questions and give your inner child a voice to respond to – Who says 'I can't,' 'I mustn't,' 'I shouldn't', "I have to', or 'What would happen if I did?'

Listen to your body's natural cycle. There are cycles in everything within the universe, so it is important to respect your body, especially for the need to rest from activity. The further you get from your natural cycle, the more stress and suffering you perceive life to be. For an efficient workday that respects your human nature is to understand your Ultradian Cycles.

* Manage your energy, not your time! Take breaks as your brain can only focus for 90-120 minutes

* Use a timer of 90-120 minutes to help monitor thought-intensive activity

* Take a screen break or rest for 20 minutes to regain alertness and renewal to achieve your next high-performance task

* Carve your workday into a trio of 90-minute windows. This helps you to move from higher to lower alertness to increase productivity, called the Ultradian Rhythm

* Change your mindset by caring less about time limits to caring more about results. Ask yourself, 'What can I achieve in 90 minutes?'

* Stop multitasking and increase the relevance of each task

* Eliminate distractors and switch off notifications from computers and phone even when one task is present

* Decide how you will rest (read, meditate, nap, healthy snack)

* Cut down on sugar and coffee. Remember, caffeine is also present in cola and chocolate. These stimulants mimic an adrenaline rush providing an energy surge but then followed by an energy dip. You want to avoid this, as stimulants also have a roller-coaster effect on your emotions

Awakening your Smartyr Self

✴

Smartyr
Self-hypnosis

How to Read the Smartyr Script Out Loud

* We recommend the minimum requirement to complete the series is to read one smartyr script each day in the same sequence for six weeks. This method works more powerfully when used regularly and with commitment

* Before you start, check-in with how you feel using the following list. Mentally scan your body and tick the boxes that best describe how you feel

* Read the script right through from start to finish, it is important you take your time because each hypnosis is purposefully repetitive which adds to the powerful relaxation and trance-like state which is needed for hypnosis

* Start reading aloud in a slow, calm, and purposeful assertive tone

* Pronounce each word fully so it feels like the message you want to convey

* Pause and take a breath where indicated by the dots within the script

* If using a metronome, set it at 50, and allow two full beats before continuing to read

* Read-aloud words written in bold, extended, and italics with emphasis and conviction

* When you finish, check-out with how you feel. Mentally scan your body and tick the boxes that best describe how you feel, compare with your check-in

* Use the journaling pages at the end of each hypnosis to support your progress, insights, thoughts, and reflections

Pre Self-hypnosis
Check-in

Negative	Despair	Angry	Insignificant
Resentful	Low	Frustrated	Suspicious
Critical	Guilty	Disapproving	Miserable
Neutral	Confused	Inquisitive	Vulnerable
Relieved	Excited	Amazed	Interested
Furious	Hopeless	Disappointed	Powerful
Stuck	Determined	Trapped	Blocked
Bitter	Unhappy	Impressed	Disgruntled
Alive	Let Down	Irritated	Anxious
Joyful	Nervous	Annoyed	Insecure
Resistant	Hesitant	Happy	Weak
Bored	Cautious	Powerless	Rejected
Content	Hopeful	Grief	Embarrassed
Curious	Inspired	Victimised	Fearful
Awful	Neglected	Optimistic	Surprised
Scared	Overwhelmed	Lonely	Creative
Inadequate	Helpless	Energetic	Heartbroken
Tense	Calm	Tired	Hesitant
Eager	Worried	Hurt	Safe
Restless	Apprehensive	Regretful	Grateful
Unsure	Judgemental	Confident	Valued
Shocked	Worthless	Thankful	Abandoned
Playful	Glad	Depressed	Withdrawn

Awakening your Smartyr Self
Smartyr Self-Hypnosis

every time I read the **words in bold**.. and with every suggestion I give myself, **will** sink in **so deeply** into the unconscious part of my mind, **now**.. feeling settled and taking in a deep breath…. I continue to focus on my breath.. I allow my body to become more settled and more relaxed.. I feel a tingling on the top of my head.. as I continue to become more and more relaxed.. I feel gently at peace.. fully at ease.. totally safe.. and perfectly secure and comfortable..

as my relaxation **deepens, now**.. I feel a wonderful sense of calmness traveling down the back of my head.. I have a sense of warmth and sense of tingling and I have become **more** and **more relaxed**.. I welcome this gentle and warm relaxation filling my body, **now**..

as I read out loud.. I can feel this sense of relaxation moving the down the front of my face.. and I feel the tiny muscles around my eyes relaxing.. my mouth relaxing.. and my jaw relaxing.. to the soothing and calming tone of my voice..

my breath is in tune with my heartbeat, making me feel a **deeper** sense of **relaxation**.. this wonderful sense of **calm**.. and peace moves down my neck and relaxes my shoulders and my chest.. as I continue to read out loud the soothing sound of my voice relaxes the rest of my body.. right to the soles of my feet.. tingling and becoming perfectly **relaxed**.. as I continue to focus on my breath…. becoming more and more **relaxed**..

every time I read the **words in bold**.. and with every suggestion I give myself, **will** sink in **so deeply** into the unconscious part of

my mind, *now*.. I see myself moving toward a wide set of well-lit stairs.. I approach this beautiful staircase.. and I am curious where it leads me.. I am surrounded by large protective panes of glass.. and I can clearly see the view.. I feel safe.. as I think about moving *up* these well-lit stairs.. I feel warm as I think about climbing *up* this stunning staircase..

as I take in the view.. I have a sense of anticipation.. as I am looking forward to moving further *up* the staircase.. I feel totally safe, perfectly secure.. as I continue to climb *up* the steps.. I momentarily pause.. taking in a *deep* breath…. I look out of the window and I see the rooftops.. they look like dolls houses.. they are fun and interesting from this view..

from this moment.. as I continue to climb *up*.. I decide to count from one to five… when I reach *five*.. I know I will be perfectly relaxed, and in my own natural state of peace and perfect relaxation.. counting *up now*..

every time I read the *words in bold*.. and with every suggestion I give myself, *will* sink in *so deeply* into the unconscious part of my mind, *now*..

One.. feeling good.. feeling fine.. gently at peace.. fully at ease.. totally safe and perfectly secure.. as I continue to focus on my breath…. I feel myself surrendering to the deep and perfect relaxation that is filling my body.. *now*..

I feel *fine*.. totally safe and perfectly secure.. moving *up*.. and yet going into a *deeper* sense of *relaxation*.. every time I say a number out loud.. it causes me to go *deeper* and *deeper* into *relaxation*..

Two.. as I continue to move *up* the stairs, I pause to look out of the window again.. taking in a *deep* breath.... *now*, I see and view the tops of the trees.. they look magnificent..

from this moment, as I continue to climb *up*.. I become more and more curious.. I feel myself becoming *more* and *more* *relaxed*.. gently at peace.. feeling good.. totally safe.. perfectly secure.. moving *up*, yet, going into a *deeper* sense of *relaxation*.. every time I say a number out loud.. it causes me to go deeper and deeper into *relaxation*..

Three.. feeling good, feeling fine.. totally safe.. perfectly secure.. as I continue to focus on my breath.... *now*, I feel myself surrendering to the deep and perfect relaxation that is filling my body.. I feel fine.. totally safe, perfectly secure.. moving *up* the stairs, yet going into a *deeper* sense of *relaxation*.. as I continue to read out loud.. every time I say a number.. it causes me to go even more deeper and *deeper* into **relaxation**.. feeling gently at peace, feeling good.. feeling fine, totally safe.. and perfectly secure..

Four.. feeling good, feeling fine.. and gently at peace.. fully at *ease*.. totally safe and perfectly secure.. as I continue to *breathe deeply*.... I feel myself surrendering to the deep and perfect relaxation, *now*.. filling my body..

as I continue to move *up* the stairs.. I pause to look out of the window again.. taking in a *deep* breath.... I am *now* in awe of the mountain peaks.. I see them glistening from the rays of the sun coming through the clouds.. they look majestic.. and they look glorious..

from this moment.. as I continue to climb *up*.. I become more and more curious as to where this is taking me.. and feel myself *more* and *more relaxed*.. gently at peace.. feeling good.. totally safe.. perfectly secure.. moving *up*, yet going into a deeper sense of relaxation.. every time I say a number out loud.. it causes me to go *deeper* and *deeper* into *relaxation*..

Five.. feeling wonder-struck and totally safe.. perfectly secure.. I take a *deep* breath…. as I have surrendered *now* to the deep and perfect *relaxation* that has *now* filled my body.. I feel fine.. totally safe and perfectly secure..

I reach the top of the staircase.. and see a warden guarding a beautiful archway.. the warden gives me a protective nod.. and I realize that it is *me* who is architect of this stunning staircase.. and it is *me* who has stationed the warden here .. for my protection..

feeling safe and perfectly secure.. I *easily* bypass the warden.. I *easily* walk out onto the balcony.. and find myself gently being in the most comfortable position.. feeling a perfect state of *relaxation*.

as I relax and focus on my breath…. I *now* find myself sitting above the clouds.. I feel completely at *ease* and I begin to feel a *beautiful sensation* of peace and relaxation, tranquility and calm.. I imagine the *ideal me* projected onto the sky like a movie screen *now*.. as I picture myself, my mind and body feels a wonderful *sense of calm*, and feels gently at peace..

I made a *good decision* to climb the staircase, as I can *now* see myself more clearly, and with a better view.. I see myself as I am.. *I Am so relaxed*.. that my mind has become so sensitive..

so receptive to what I read out loud.. that every time I read the *words in bold*.. and with every suggestion I give myself, *will* sink in *so deeply* into the unconscious part of my mind.. that it will begin to cause such a *lasting impression* there, *now*..

tranquility and calm are flowing through my mind and body like a cool breeze, giving me such a pleasant feeling.. such a beautiful sensation… as I embed positive suggestions into my unconscious mind, I *now* acknowledge *my true value*.. these suggestions exercise a greater and *greater influence* to the way I think.. over the way I feel.. over the way I behave.. and the way *I become smartyr*.

every time I read the *words in bold*.. and with every suggestion *I give myself,* will sink in so deeply.. into the unconscious part of my mind.. that it will begin to cause such a *lasting impression, now*.. and *will* remain firmly embedded in the unconscious part of my mind, *now*.. even after I have stopped reading out loud..

I feel good that *I am* interested in improving my life.. and.. just *now*.. *I am* finding ways to develop my smartyr self. *I am committed* to the dedication of my practice to moderate my emotional state..

now.. drifting deeper and deeper all the time as I continue to listen to my voice.. I *hear my voice*, I slow down, I drift deeper and deeper.. I feel a wonderful sense of calm..

now.. I continue to develop the skill and capacity to moderate my emotional state.. while *I focus* what happens in my body, *now*.. I have the means to *filter my thoughts and my feelings*..

I have developed my internal self-moderator, *now*.. I do not need to second guess what I do, or say.. I have practiced the art of *self-control* and *I can respond in a positive way*.. I rarely regret anything I have said..

as a smartyr.. I have cultivated a sense of Self.. *I am aware* enough that I can take personal responsibility, *now*.. *I am good* at regulating my own subjective experience.. *I have learned* the ability to respond rather than react..

I can reflectively self-function.. which means I can *now*.. think about my feelings, and feel about my thinking.. from this knowing, *I can choose* to manage my emotional states *now*.. and my behavior.. *I can set clear boundaries* for myself and for others.. because *I can set clear boundaries*, *now*.. I am able to avoid impulsive reactions that I may later regret.. because I can consider what needs to be said.. I consider if it needs to be said by me.. and *I can* consider if it is appropriate to be said by me at the time..

now.. *I am skilful* at knowing when to engage with impulsivity and spontaneity without later regretting my actions, *now*.. *I know what is good for me*.. I know what my limitations are.. I know how to regulate and *now*.. *I look after myself with compassion*..

these suggestions will continue to influence and become part of my natural inner dialogue as I go about my day.. every day I will become so deeply interested in whatever *I am doing*.. whatever *I am feeling*.. whatever *I am thinking*.. and whatever is going on around me.. that my mind will be in a state of relaxation..

I am.. going to *feel physically stronger* and.. I will *feel more alert*.. more wide awake.. *more energetic*.. and much less easily discouraged..

I will wake up from my self-hypnotic trance by counting to three.. while reading out-loud.. when I get to number *three*.. I will be wide awake, fully alert, and will be *feeling better than ever before*..

Three.. feeling *satisfied* and *proud*, I am beginning to awaken from my hypnotic trance..

Two. becoming aware of my body, *I am excited* about the positive results from this session..

ONE, ONE, ONE, now, wide awake, refreshed and *feeling better than ever before!*

Post Hypnosis Reflections

* Check-out with how you feel using the following list. Mentally scan your body and tick the boxes that best describe how you feel
* Your results will vary depending on your regularity and repetition on completing the series
* Journal any thoughts, feelings or insights that may emerge on the following pages
* Notice, observe and feel into the subtle shifts in your daily interactions as this is the trajectory for preferable life changes to eventually occur

Post Self-hypnosis
Check-out

Negative	Despair	Angry	Insignificant
Resentful	Low	Frustrated	Suspicious
Critical	Guilty	Disapproving	Miserable
Neutral	Confused	Inquisitive	Vulnerable
Relieved	Excited	Amazed	Interested
Furious	Hopeless	Disappointed	Powerful
Stuck	Determined	Trapped	Blocked
Bitter	Unhappy	Impressed	Disgruntled
Alive	Let Down	Irritated	Anxious
Joyful	Nervous	Annoyed	Insecure
Resistant	Hesitant	Happy	Weak
Bored	Cautious	Powerless	Rejected
Content	Hopeful	Grief	Embarrassed
Curious	Inspired	Victimised	Fearful
Awful	Neglected	Optimistic	Surprised
Scared	Overwhelmed	Lonely	Creative
Inadequate	Helpless	Energetic	Heartbroken
Tense	Calm	Tired	Hesitant
Eager	Worried	Hurt	Safe
Restless	Apprehensive	Regretful	Grateful
Unsure	Judgemental	Confident	Valued
Shocked	Worthless	Thankful	Abandoned
Playful	Glad	Depressed	Withdrawn

Journaling
Insights - Thoughts - Reflections

Journaling
Insights - Thoughts - Reflections

Understanding Intrinsic Motivation

Chapter 22

Understanding Intrinsic Motivation

Intrinsic motivation means fulfilling and achieving visions and goals based on internal factors. In other words, our deeply held wants and desires to stimulate our self-motivation.

Motivation comes from the root word 'to move.' It is a temporary state that is felt physically in the body and mind. It is dynamic, and its processes arouse, maintain, and drives behavior to create a plan of action. You will use your deepest emotions to move and guide you towards your goals. When you feel a sense of achievement, you become invigorated and energized. Your reward system reinforces a sequence of successful behaviors in you.

The outcome is stored in your long-term memory and recalled at later times when needed. Synapses in your brain strengthen and create a reinforced positive loop, driving further motivation forward. It is paramount that you become adept in self-moderation. Exercising the ability to respond to your emotional and behavioral reactions will help create the potentiality of your success and achievement. To do that, you need to discover your personal value system. As you move towards smartyrdom, your values will begin to reveal themselves to you through aspiration and inspiration.

When you focus positively, your motivated behavior will highlight the recognition of a need. These action-seeking rewards are naturally satisfying, like developing healthy habits, a need for accomplishment, building stronger relationships, developing a passion, the need to co-create, and actualizing your creativity or a desire to belong and be accepted by the wider community.

People are naturally driven by a need to grow and gain fulfilment, and it is this need for growth that will drive you towards smartyrdom. You recognize that motivation and self-determination is the prerequisite to your success. As a smartyr, you understand your enthusiasm as being the ambitious force that motivates you into action and to pursue your goals. You will be full of self-appreciation, liking yourself enough for the thoughts you are thinking and for the things you are doing. Primarily, this ability plays an essential role in your psychological health and wellbeing.

To develop your smartyr Self, you need to understand the difference between extrinsic and intrinsic motivation. People who pay more attention to external rewards such as money earned, recognition gained, and others' validation are extrinsically motivated. Their behavior is driven by a desire to gain an external reward that is not necessarily related to a more profound sense of satisfaction or meaning.

In other words, if your motivation for reading this book is about a general understanding of psychology, then it is considered extrinsic motivation. In contrast, if your motivation is for true personal growth, to develop a better version of yourself, reading this book is regarded as intrinsic motivation. It is about internal satisfaction and being in your element at doing something for pure enjoyment or to create positive emotions within yourself that give you a sense of meaning and progress. When you are intrinsically motivated, you take action that is naturally creative, full of enthusiasm, and driven by self-determination. It is only then that extrinsic rewards are enjoyed as a natural byproduct rather than a goal.

Life is continuous progress, and there are different stages of readiness for inner work. It does not matter if you recognize your motivation as currently extrinsic. We want you to consider your motivation for reading this book to be an intrinsic one and for the need to gain mastery over personal challenges and find the incentive to take in new experiences essential for developing a cohesive sense of Self.

When you focus primarily on your intrinsic motivation, it actively directs you towards your internal growth cultivating self-knowledge and independence. You can be motivated towards reaching a long-term goal, such as raising your self-esteem. Perhaps a shorter and more straightforward goal, such as saying no to an event you are expected to attend. Your intrinsic motivation has the incentive, desire, and willingness to initiate and support you to persevere in the face of setbacks.

Procrastination

Procrastination can be the killer of all your opportunities. Therefore, it would be unkind to judge procrastination as being lazy. Instead, you might be unconsciously avoiding the fear of failure, success, or avoiding making future-oriented decisions when stressed. On the flip side, procrastination can also unconsciously create space to think and build momentum for something new or different to emerge. It is only when procrastination becomes part of your martyr identity, you experience feeling stuck and lacking in motivation. As a martyr, you are fundamentally unhappy as your passiveness renders you stuck and feeling blocked in your life. Therefore, reasons for not living the life you want are due to an absence of purpose, enthusiasm, and passion. This can leave you lacking the motivation to drive and pursue matters, ultimately procrastination, and the cycle begins again.

Induced Motivation

When you become a smartyr, you trust the divine timing of things; therefore, you do not blame others when you lack enthusiasm for action and when in pursuit of your goals. You have come to realize that action is provoked by your determination, enthusiasm, trust in the divine timing, along with the engagement of your internal self-moderator. You are self-determined in finding ways to motivate yourself to maintain what we call 'induced motivation.'

This kind of motivation is not artificial. It is authentic and sincere. You create an awareness of your physiological and psychological impressions that influence your levels of enthusiasm, determination, and motivation for a positive outcome.

As humans, we naturally seek practices that bring us fulfilment. Therefore, having a set of principles or ideals will drive your motivation and guide your behavior. When motivation emerges, insight into your internal value system and the principles you stand for becomes evident.

The smartyr knows what gives their life meaning. They know what is important to them, what they value, and why they value it, and because of this, they see the precedence it has in their life. Once you become a smartyr, the outcome will provide you with a purpose and direction to determine and drive your internal motivation.

If you are currently finding it difficult to motivate yourself, consider what you are doing has no genuine desire. Then it is time to discover what you truly want. Consider some fundamental components of life that would include passion, vocation, profession, and mission.

Considerations

Ask yourself the following questions to help stimulate intrinsic motivation in you:

* How does what I love meet what I am good at?
* How does what I am good at meet what can be valued?
* How does what I value and get paid for meet what the world needs?

You will connect to your spiritual realm once you have identified your internal value system and live by it. How you grow as a person and your choices for your personal development, and the amount you actually like yourself when with others and when alone, along with the qualities of being honest, self-disciplined, and being true to your word, will raise your self-esteem and enhance your overall sense of happiness.

When motivation is induced by an internal factor and intrinsically motivated, you will find yourself in flow and you will have the energy to keep going even in the face of obstacles. Engaging with the following questions will help you connect with desired visions and executing tangible goals.

Here are some questions to help you explore explicit desires and assist in setting your intentions.

* When are you most in your element?
* What activity do you engage in that makes time fly?
* What is it you do you that you find easy or natural?
* Do you enjoy most activities on your own or with others?
* What do you love doing so much that you would do it for free?
* What interests and excites you that it gives you energy?
* What did you like doing when you were a child?

Explore what is important about each of them. Free flow your expression as you write and consider doing this with your non-dominate hand. Your deepest motivations are likely to surface once you have exhausted the process, so keep going and dig deep into the crevices of your creative thoughts.

Prioritize and list your values. Your values determine how you spend your time. You will probably devote significant time to the top few on your list.

This exercise is essential to help avoid conflicts within your value system; otherwise, it could get in the way of achieving your goals.

* List your values on paper
* Cut the list into strips

* Ask yourself, 'if I can only choose one, which one is it?'
* Remove it from the line-up. This is your top priority
* Return to what is left and repeat until all the value strips are now placed in order of priority.

Question your values. This helps you gauge a deeper understanding of the effects on your wellbeing, relationships, and social factors and how they are embedded in your attitudes and behavior.

From your list of priorities, ask yourself, 'Why is that important?' This will help decipher if your motivation is towards or away from each value.

* I love the choice and freedom of being self-employed – this is a 'towards' answer which induces extrinsic motivation and helps you achieve your goal. It is the invigorating and energizing drive of motivation
* Because it is better than working for someone – this is an 'away' answer which is directionless and eventually loses its momentum
* Focus on what you want and not what you do not want by asking the above same questions to each value you list.

Make goals. Goals are guided by your intrinsic and extrinsic motivation and are the desired end-state. Its outcome can leave you feeling satisfied, full of pride, and stable – it will give you meaning and a sense of having order and structure in your life.

* Establish goals that raise interest as they carry you from one experience to the next

* Check if the goal renews your energy levels when you think about it, rate it out of 10
* Make your goal compelling as it will add value and drive motivation
* Visualize achieving your goal by engaging with the read-aloud smartyr self-hypnosis
* Imagine that you have already reached it. Notice how this makes you feel
* Make this image big and colorful
* Meditate on its color, how it moves and how it sounds
* Step into the picture, so your good feeling gets stronger, and notice how positive that feels
* Step back out of the image and see your goal ahead of you. This will motivate you to get there.

Set a date when you wish to achieve your goal. If you do not specify your goal it will become vague, and it is highly likely it will never happen.

* Write a specific date in your diary when you will start
* Write a specific date in your journal when your goal will be complete
* Create a timeline and break down your main goal into smaller achievable ones
* Diarize these small milestones to support the process
* Plan a small reward for each milestone achieved
* Decide in advance how you will reward yourself when you reach the outcome

* Stay focused on the bigger picture when you find yourself feeling either overwhelmed or demotivated. Managing the day-to-day stuff can become boring and tedious
* Take time out and repeat your read-aloud smartyr self-hypnosis
* Take time out and create a vision board by collating images to stimulate the senses of your desired outcome.

Journaling
Insights - Thoughts - Reflections

Intrinsic Motivation

✴

Smartyr
Self-hypnosis

How to Read the Smartyr Script Out Loud

* We recommend the minimum requirement to complete the series is to read one smartyr script each day in the same sequence for six weeks. This method works more powerfully when used regularly and with commitment

* Before you start, check-in with how you feel using the following list. Mentally scan your body and tick the boxes that best describe how you feel

* Read the script right through from start to finish, it is important you take your time because each hypnosis is purposefully repetitive which adds to the powerful relaxation and trance-like state which is needed for hypnosis

* Start reading aloud in a slow, calm, and purposeful assertive tone

* Pronounce each word fully so it feels like the message you want to convey

* Pause and take a breath where indicated by the dots within the script

* If using a metronome, set it at 50, and allow two full beats before continuing to read

* Read-aloud words written in bold, extended, and italics with emphasis and conviction

* When you finish, check-out with how you feel. Mentally scan your body and tick the boxes that best describe how you feel, compare with your check-in

* Use the journaling pages at the end of each hypnosis to support your progress, insights, thoughts, and reflections

Pre Self-hypnosis
Check-in

Negative	Despair	Angry	Insignificant
Resentful	Low	Frustrated	Suspicious
Critical	Guilty	Disapproving	Miserable
Neutral	Confused	Inquisitive	Vulnerable
Relieved	Excited	Amazed	Interested
Furious	Hopeless	Disappointed	Powerful
Stuck	Determined	Trapped	Blocked
Bitter	Unhappy	Impressed	Disgruntled
Alive	Let Down	Irritated	Anxious
Joyful	Nervous	Annoyed	Insecure
Resistant	Hesitant	Happy	Weak
Bored	Cautious	Powerless	Rejected
Content	Hopeful	Grief	Embarrassed
Curious	Inspired	Victimised	Fearful
Awful	Neglected	Optimistic	Surprised
Scared	Overwhelmed	Lonely	Creative
Inadequate	Helpless	Energetic	Heartbroken
Tense	Calm	Tired	Hesitant
Eager	Worried	Hurt	Safe
Restless	Apprehensive	Regretful	Grateful
Unsure	Judgemental	Confident	Valued
Shocked	Worthless	Thankful	Abandoned
Playful	Glad	Depressed	Withdrawn

Intrinsic Motivation
Smartyr Self-Hypnosis

every time I read the **words in bold..** and with every suggestion I give myself, **will** sink in **so deeply** into the unconscious part of my mind, **now..** feeling settled and taking in a deep breath.... I continue to focus on my breath.. I allow my body to become more settled and more relaxed.. I feel a tingling on the top of my head.. as I continue to become more and more relaxed.. I feel gently at peace.. fully at ease.. totally safe.. and perfectly secure and comfortable..

as my relaxation **deepens, now..** I feel a wonderful sense of calmness traveling down the back of my head.. I have a sense of warmth and sense of tingling and I have become **more** and **more relaxed..** I welcome this gentle and warm relaxation filling my body, **now..**

as I read out loud.. I can feel this sense of relaxation moving the down the front of my face.. and I feel the tiny muscles around my eyes relaxing.. my mouth relaxing.. and my jaw relaxing.. to the soothing and calming tone of my voice..

my breath is in tune with my heartbeat, making me feel a **deeper** sense of **relaxation..** this wonderful sense of **calm..** and peace moves down my neck and relaxes my shoulders and my chest.. as I continue to read out loud the soothing sound of my voice relaxes the rest of my body.. right to the soles of my feet.. tingling and becoming perfectly **relaxed..** as I continue to focus on my breath.... becoming more and more **relaxed..**

every time I read the **words in bold..** and with every suggestion I give myself, **will** sink in **so deeply** into the unconscious part of my mind, *now*.. I see myself moving toward a wide set of well–lit stairs.. I approach this beautiful staircase.. and I am curious where it leads me.. I am surrounded by large protective panes of glass.. and I can clearly see the view.. I feel safe.. as I think about moving *up* these well–lit stairs.. I feel warm as I think about climbing *up* this stunning staircase..

as I take in the view.. I have a sense of anticipation.. as I am looking forward to moving further *up* the staircase.. I feel totally safe, perfectly secure.. as I continue to climb *up* the steps.. I momentarily pause.. taking in a *deep* breath…. I look out of the window and I see the rooftops.. they look like dolls houses.. they are fun and interesting from this view..

from this moment.. as I continue to climb *up*.. I decide to count from one to five… when I reach *five*.. I know I will be perfectly relaxed, and in my own natural state of peace and perfect relaxation.. counting *up now*..

every time I read the *words in bold*.. and with every suggestion I give myself, *will* sink in *so deeply* into the unconscious part of my mind, *now*..

One.. feeling good.. feeling fine.. gently at peace.. fully at ease.. totally safe and perfectly secure.. as I continue to focus on my breath…. I feel myself surrendering to the deep and perfect relaxation that is filling my body.. *now*..

I feel *fine*.. totally safe and perfectly secure.. moving *up*.. and yet going into a *deeper* sense of *relaxation*.. every time I say a number out loud.. it causes me to go *deeper* and *deeper* into *relaxation*..

Two.. as I continue to move *up* the stairs, I pause to look out of the window again.. taking in a *deep* breath.... *now*, I see and view the tops of the trees.. they look magnificent..

from this moment, as I continue to climb *up*.. I become more and more curious.. I feel myself becoming *more* and *more* *relaxed*.. gently at peace.. feeling good.. totally safe.. perfectly secure.. moving *up*, yet, going into a *deeper* sense of *relaxation*.. every time I say a number out loud.. it causes me to go deeper and deeper into *relaxation*..

Three.. feeling good, feeling fine.. totally safe.. perfectly secure.. as I continue to focus on my breath.... *now*, I feel myself surrendering to the deep and perfect relaxation that is filling my body.. I feel fine.. totally safe, perfectly secure.. moving *up* the stairs, yet going into a *deeper* sense of *relaxation*.. as I continue to read out loud.. every time I say a number.. it causes me to go even more deeper and *deeper* into **relaxation**.. feeling gently at peace, feeling good.. feeling fine, totally safe.. and perfectly secure..

Four.. feeling good, feeling fine.. and gently at peace.. fully at *ease*.. totally safe and perfectly secure.. as I continue to *breathe deeply*.... I feel myself surrendering to the deep and perfect relaxation, *now*.. filling my body..

as I continue to move *up* the stairs.. I pause to look out of the window again.. taking in a *deep* breath.... I am *now* in awe of the mountain peaks.. I see them glistening from the rays of the sun coming through the clouds.. they look majestic.. and they look glorious..

from this moment.. as I continue to climb **up**.. I become more and more curious as to where this is taking me.. and feel myself **more** and **more relaxed**.. gently at peace.. feeling good.. totally safe.. perfectly secure.. moving **up**, yet going into a deeper sense of relaxation.. every time I say a number out loud.. it causes me to go **deeper** and **deeper** into **relaxation**..

Five.. feeling wonder–struck and totally safe.. perfectly secure.. I take a **deep** breath…. as I have surrendered **now** to the deep and perfect **relaxation** that has **now** filled my body.. I feel fine.. totally safe and perfectly secure..

I reach the top of the staircase.. and see a warden guarding a beautiful archway.. the warden gives me a protective nod.. and I realize that it is **me** who is architect of this stunning staircase.. and it is **me** who has stationed the warden here .. for my protection..

feeling safe and perfectly secure.. I **easily** bypass the warden.. I **easily** walk out onto the balcony.. and find myself gently being in the most comfortable position.. feeling a perfect state of **relaxation**.

as I relax and focus on my breath…. I **now** find myself sitting above the clouds.. I feel completely at **ease** and I begin to feel a **beautiful sensation** of peace and relaxation, tranquility and calm.. I imagine the **ideal me** projected onto the sky like a movie screen **now**.. as I picture myself, my mind and body feels a wonderful **sense of calm**, and feels gently at peace..

I made a **good decision** to climb the staircase, as I can **now** see myself more clearly, and with a better view.. I see myself as I am.. **I Am so relaxed**.. that my mind has become so sensitive..

so receptive to what I read out loud.. that every time I read the *words in bold*.. and with every suggestion I give myself, *will* sink in *so deeply* into the unconscious part of my mind.. that it will begin to cause such a *lasting impression* there, *now*..

tranquility and calm are flowing through my mind and body like a cool breeze, giving me such a pleasant feeling.. such a beautiful sensation… as I embed positive suggestions into my unconscious mind, I *now* acknowledge *my true value*.. these suggestions exercise a greater and *greater influence* to the way I think.. over the way I feel.. over the way I behave.. and the way *I become smartyr*.

every time I read the *words in bold*.. and with every suggestion *I give myself,* will sink in so deeply.. into the unconscious part of my mind.. that it will begin to cause such a *lasting impression*, *now*.. and *will* remain firmly embedded in the unconscious part of my mind, *now*.. even after I have stopped reading out loud..

I feel good that *I am* interested in improving my life.. and.. just *now*.. *I am* finding ways to develop my smartyr self.. *I recognize my motivation*.. and my self-determination.. and I know these attributes are the prerequisite to my success.. I am focused on fulfilling as *I achieve my visions and goals*..

now.. drifting deeper and deeper all the time as I continue to listen to my voice.. I *hear my voice*, I slow down, I drift deeper and deeper.. I feel a wonderful sense of calm..

now.. my intrinsic motivation means *I am naturally driven* by a need to grow and gain fulfilment.. my enthusiasm for my growth drives me to become smartyr.. this desire actively directs me towards my growth, *I acquire self-knowledge*.. *I feel independent* and *I build stronger relationships*..

I know, when I procrastinate, *I am creating* space to think.. *I am building* momentum for something new and different to emerge, *now*.. my intrinsic motivation.. has the incentive.. the desire.. and willingness to initiate and.. *now* support me to persevere in the face of setbacks..

my deeply held wants and desires stimulate self–motivation and my creativity naturally follows, *now*.. *my motivation is dynamic*.. it arouses.. it maintains.. and drives my behavior.. *now*..

I know how to use my deepest emotions to move and guide me towards my goals, *now*.. I feel a sense of *achievement*.. I am *invigorated*.. I am *energised*.. and I am *motivated*.. I create plans of action..

now.. *my actions* are naturally rewarding and satisfying.. *my actions* encourage my healthy habits.. *my actions* motivate my need for accomplishment.. and.. *my actions* actualise my creativity..

I am intuitive at knowing what I love.. and.. how it meets what I am good at.. *I am smart* at knowing what I am good at.. and how that meets what can be valued.. *I am wise* at knowing how I get paid for doing what I value.. while it meet the needs of the world.. *I am an action–oriented smartyr*..

these suggestions will continue to influence and become part of my natural inner dialogue as I go about my day.. every day I will become so deeply interested in whatever *I am doing*.. whatever *I am feeling*.. whatever *I am thinking*.. and whatever is going on around me.. that my mind will be in a state of relaxation..

I am.. going to *feel physically stronger* and.. I will *feel more alert*.. more wide awake.. *more energetic*.. and much less easily discouraged..

I will wake up from my self-hypnotic trance by counting to three.. while reading out-loud.. when I get to number *three*.. I will be wide awake, fully alert, and will be *feeling better than ever before*..

Three.. feeling *satisfied* and *proud*, I am beginning to awaken from my hypnotic trance..

Two. becoming aware of my body, *I am excited* about the positive results from this session..

ONE, ONE, ONE, now, wide awake, refreshed and *feeling better than ever before!*

Post Hypnosis Reflections

* Check-out with how you feel using the following list. Mentally scan your body and tick the boxes that best describe how you feel
* Your results will vary depending on your regularity and repetition on completing the series
* Journal any thoughts, feelings or insights that may emerge on the following pages
* Notice, observe and feel into the subtle shifts in your daily interactions as this is the trajectory for preferable life changes to eventually occur

Post Self-hypnosis
Check-out

Negative		Despair		Angry		Insignificant	
Resentful		Low		Frustrated		Suspicious	
Critical		Guilty		Disapproving		Miserable	
Neutral		Confused		Inquisitive		Vulnerable	
Relieved		Excited		Amazed		Interested	
Furious		Hopeless		Disappointed		Powerful	
Stuck		Determined		Trapped		Blocked	
Bitter		Unhappy		Impressed		Disgruntled	
Alive		Let Down		Irritated		Anxious	
Joyful		Nervous		Annoyed		Insecure	
Resistant		Hesitant		Happy		Weak	
Bored		Cautious		Powerless		Rejected	
Content		Hopeful		Grief		Embarrassed	
Curious		Inspired		Victimised		Fearful	
Awful		Neglected		Optimistic		Surprised	
Scared		Overwhelmed		Lonely		Creative	
Inadequate		Helpless		Energetic		Heartbroken	
Tense		Calm		Tired		Hesitant	
Eager		Worried		Hurt		Safe	
Restless		Apprehensive		Regretful		Grateful	
Unsure		Judgemental		Confident		Valued	
Shocked		Worthless		Thankful		Abandoned	
Playful		Glad		Depressed		Withdrawn	

Journaling
Insights - Thoughts - Reflections

Journaling
Insights - Thoughts - Reflections

Cultivating Smartyr Empathy

Chapter 23

Cultivating Smartyr Empathy

Empathy is a complex concept to describe a wide range of experiences. For empathy to be effective, as a smartyr, you will maintain a distinction between yourself and another person. You will also not confuse sympathy with empathy. You will know that sympathy involves the experience of taking part in someone else's feelings. In other words, you are feeling 'for' the person whereas, when you empathize, you will know you are feeling 'with' the other person.

Most people would identify themselves as having empathy or being empathically available for others, however being empathic does not come naturally to some. It will require a deep expression from your own felt sense towards another to accurately reflect your understanding of another person's feeling state or situation.

Empathy is a paradox and is an undervalued skill that can be used insufficiently. It is what we do with empathy that makes the difference. Empathy is regarded as a social and emotional skill that helps us feel and understand others' emotions, situations, intentions, thoughts, and needs. However, when used sufficiently and skilfully, empathy provides sensitive, perceptive, and appropriate communication in support for Self and others. These attributes are known as emotion regulation, a term used to describe a person's ability to effectively manage and respond to an emotional experience.

Being empathic is much more meaningful than simply having empathy. When empathy is accurately conveyed, it is known as 'effective empathy.' It is compassion with the ability to respond to the unique experience of oneself and the other. The paradoxical aspect is that it can be used for both helpful and unhelpful purposes. For instance, as a martyr, you may use your empathy in a very sophisticated way, as an unconscious form of manipulation to get your needs met and avoid taking personal responsibility. It is a negative use of empathy that will keep you in victimhood. We are all empathic but have varying degrees of ability to apply it as a useful and positive skill in social interactions.

As a smartyr, you will have come to realize that compassion is among the greatest of virtues, aspired as the noblest quality of the human heart. Empathy is described as a compassionate action, and smartyrs know that putting empathy into action is an art that is worth practicing. Smartyrs actively strengthen their abilities to express different types of empathy as part of their everyday living.

As a smartyr, you will have honed the ability to understand another person's emotional state and oneself simultaneously. You will take moments and use your compassion and curiosity to suspend judgment towards yourself and others. You will know that empathic responses require patience, willpower, and deliberate discipline.

As a smartyr, you will recognize and appreciate that empathy is fundamental to understanding and bonding with others.

Empathy has become instrumental in your life for unravelling difficult relationships and, most profoundly, the key component to having successful relationships. It helps you understand others' perspectives, needs, and intentions.

Learning to attune to others largely depends on your early experience in receiving empathy and attunement from your early caregivers. Troubled caregivers hold up a 'cracked' mirror to the child, and their self-image forms to the cracks they see. Suppose early life has been chaotic filled with neglect and resentment. In that case, the infant grows up making this their 'normal.' They have no way of knowing that their experience has been distorted and warped by bad 'mirroring.'

In comparison, when caregivers show empathic concern when the child is either emotionally or physically wounded, the empathically attuned caregiver will tend to the child's needs until they have assimilated their experience. The child heals from taking in the feeling of acceptance that they are understood and therefore gains confidence from having a clear and genuine mirror reflected back to them.

In the film To Kill a Mockingbird, Atticus attended to Scout when she ran from the dinner table. She was scolded by their nanny for shaming a boy from school who was a guest at dinner. Scout ran out to the porch, and Atticus followed. He sat beside her, wrapped his arm around her, held her close, and tenderly listened to her as she expressed her troubles from her first day at school. He listened carefully and responded thoughtfully, reflecting her point of view while they swayed on the porch swing. Once Scout's felt-sense experience was validated, she was then able to bounce back and quickly return to dinner, where she re-engaged with her brother and their guest.

In early development, if the child experiences consistent good mirroring, it creates a secure attachment. A healthy inner life flourishes and empathy becomes readily accessible to pass on and express to others.

Atticus also told Scout that the teacher was new, and it was her first day at school. He explained to her, "If you learn this single trick, you'll get along a lot better with all kinds of folks." He then added, "You never really understand a single person until you consider things from his point of view… till you climb inside of his skin and walk around in it", then proceeded to make a compromise to which she agreed.

His perceptive engagement and compassion gave him the capacity to accurately identify the emotions in Scout and at the same time show concern for her teacher and their guest at dinner.

So, in the words of Atticus, you as a smartyr recognizes that understanding your own emotions will help you get along better "with all kinds of folks."

Considerations

Here are some tips to help sense and respond to the emotions in others.

The first stage is to gather valuable information on what you visually notice the person may be feeling. This exercise momentarily places the focus away from you and puts it on the other person.

Observe and pay attention to what you see

* One skill of becoming empathic is to consciously pay attention to the subtle changes in a person's emotional state. Paying attention to the nuances of facial expressions, posture, and body movements, breathing patterns, skin color changes, and muscle tension.

Observe and pay attention to what you hear

* Avoid listening only to the 'words' the person uses. Listening to the tone and quality of their voice, pitch, volume, and tempo will tell you a lot about a person's emotional state.

Notice if the person lacks in emotional expression

* Listen for dry or abstract language or a monotone voice. These observations inform you the person may not be in touch with their feelings and may not be conscious of this fact.

Register keywords and phrases used

* The words and phrases a person use have an essential effect on the view they have of themselves. Words like 'I can't, it's impossible, I am sorry' show feelings of powerlessness and worthlessness. Words like 'I should, I have to, I must' mean they feel duty-bound to do things they do not want to do, which is also tied into their worthlessness.

The second stage is an inward inquiry into your responses from the information you have gathered.

These exercises place the focus on yourself in relation to the other person.

What image does the person's words evoke in you?

* Words or metaphors another person uses inform what is on their mind and can trigger images in your mind. Notice how these images make you feel. Are they positive and empowering, or are they upsetting and draining?

Imagine standing in the other person's shoes

* Try and see things from the other person's perspective. It is helpful to imagine you are them. If you practice being them, talk using their words, stand or walk as they do and breathe as they breathe, and you will feel what they feel. Experiencing their perspective helps you to empathize with their experiences, challenges, and thought processes. This is effective when used both positively and negatively.

Develop an inward inquiry to your emotional responses

* Sometimes you get a feeling from someone. It could be that you have unconsciously picked up information about how the other person feels. However, first, inwardly check you are not projecting your feelings into the situation. Learning to differentiate feelings between you and another can be tricky, so it would

be useful to understand the phenomena of projection, which will be explained below.

Projection

It is human nature to keep yourself safe and protected against painful and negative feelings and experiences. Suppose you notice a sudden reaction in response to something you have said or done; you are likely to have slipped into the phenomena of projection. This unconscious phenomenon is about pushing out the disowned parts of yourself onto and into others. By disowning those parts of yourself, you think you are protecting yourself, but instead, you have projected.

You have unconsciously pushed out the uncomfortable and disowned thoughts and feelings that belong to you. You transpose what affects your impulses and ideas onto the other person and distort how you see and experience them. It inevitably renders you to judgment and attack and conveys that you are the better person in your relationships.

As projection is mainly done out of awareness, you are convinced you have kept yourself safe from attack. Unknowingly and undeniably, the projection will always hurt you. Projection and attack are inevitably related because projection is always the means of justifying an attack.

If you ignore the phenomena of projection, you will not only continue to unconsciously hurt yourself, but you also destroy the reality of both yourself and others. You will fail to see the truth of the relational dynamic, and you will fail to see and experience the person for who they really are. Therefore, projection is the absence of empathy and compassion, and it is not the healthiest way to deal with emotions. It is a difficult habit or a pattern of relating to break, especially if you are in martyrdom.

As a smartyr, you can accept your failings and weaknesses. You can deal with the monsters in your head rather than project the negative emotions you are experiencing onto and into others. You will expand your own empathic potential towards yourself and give yourself healthy options when dealing with difficult emotions. You cultivate to improve your life quality and tolerate recognizing and experiencing the negatives about yourself. You, therefore, tend not to project and obscure your equality with others.

Cultivating the capacity to understand other people's thoughts and feelings and putting empathy into practice increases your self-awareness. It becomes a powerful driver that strengthens your relationships and motivates you to create close friendships and caring communities.

Empathy leads you along the way to intimate, long-lasting relationships and motivates you to acts of compassion and altruism. It adds immeasurably to the complexity and wonder of life. It helps you understand people who might at first seem strange or unlovable.

When you expand your perspective and open your mind to empathy, it adds a necessary element of social and moral behavior, taking you deep into the heart of what it means to be human.

Journaling
Insights - Thoughts - Reflections

Cultivate Empathy
&
Self-Compassion

✳

Smartyr
Self-hypnosis

How to Read the Smartyr Script Out Loud

* We recommend the minimum requirement to complete the series is to read one smartyr script each day in the same sequence for six weeks. This method works more powerfully when used regularly and with commitment

* Before you start, check-in with how you feel using the following list. Mentally scan your body and tick the boxes that best describe how you feel

* Read the script right through from start to finish, it is important you take your time because each hypnosis is purposefully repetitive which adds to the powerful relaxation and trance-like state which is needed for hypnosis

* Start reading aloud in a slow, calm, and purposeful assertive tone

* Pronounce each word fully so it feels like the message you want to convey

* Pause and take a breath where indicated by the dots within the script

* If using a metronome, set it at 50, and allow two full beats before continuing to read

* Read-aloud words written in bold, extended, and italics with emphasis and conviction

* When you finish, check-out with how you feel. Mentally scan your body and tick the boxes that best describe how you feel, compare with your check-in

* Use the journaling pages at the end of each hypnosis to support your progress, insights, thoughts, and reflections

Pre Self-hypnosis
Check-in

Negative	Despair	Angry	Insignificant
Resentful	Low	Frustrated	Suspicious
Critical	Guilty	Disapproving	Miserable
Neutral	Confused	Inquisitive	Vulnerable
Relieved	Excited	Amazed	Interested
Furious	Hopeless	Disappointed	Powerful
Stuck	Determined	Trapped	Blocked
Bitter	Unhappy	Impressed	Disgruntled
Alive	Let Down	Irritated	Anxious
Joyful	Nervous	Annoyed	Insecure
Resistant	Hesitant	Happy	Weak
Bored	Cautious	Powerless	Rejected
Content	Hopeful	Grief	Embarrassed
Curious	Inspired	Victimised	Fearful
Awful	Neglected	Optimistic	Surprised
Scared	Overwhelmed	Lonely	Creative
Inadequate	Helpless	Energetic	Heartbroken
Tense	Calm	Tired	Hesitant
Eager	Worried	Hurt	Safe
Restless	Apprehensive	Regretful	Grateful
Unsure	Judgemental	Confident	Valued
Shocked	Worthless	Thankful	Abandoned
Playful	Glad	Depressed	Withdrawn

Cultivate Empathy & Self-Compassion Smartyr Self-Hypnosis

every time I read the ***words in bold..*** and with every suggestion I give myself, ***will*** sink in ***so deeply*** into the unconscious part of my mind, ***now..*** feeling settled and taking in a deep breath…. I continue to focus on my breath.. I allow my body to become more settled and more relaxed.. I feel a tingling on the top of my head.. as I continue to become more and more relaxed.. I feel gently at peace.. fully at ease.. totally safe.. and perfectly secure and comfortable..

as my relaxation ***deepens, now..*** I feel a wonderful sense of calmness traveling down the back of my head.. I have a sense of warmth and sense of tingling and I have become ***more*** and ***more relaxed..*** I welcome this gentle and warm relaxation filling my body, ***now..***

as I read out loud.. I can feel this sense of relaxation moving the down the front of my face.. and I feel the tiny muscles around my eyes relaxing.. my mouth relaxing.. and my jaw relaxing.. to the soothing and calming tone of my voice..

my breath is in tune with my heartbeat, making me feel a ***deeper*** sense of ***relaxation..*** this wonderful sense of ***calm..*** and peace moves down my neck and relaxes my shoulders and my chest.. as I continue to read out loud the soothing sound of my voice relaxes the rest of my body.. right to the soles of my feet.. tingling and becoming perfectly ***relaxed..*** as I continue to focus on my breath…. becoming more and more ***relaxed..***

every time I read the ***words in bold..*** and with every suggestion I give myself, ***will*** sink in ***so deeply*** into the unconscious part of my mind, **now**.. I see myself moving toward a wide set of well-lit stairs.. I approach this beautiful staircase.. and I am curious where it leads me.. I am surrounded by large protective panes of glass.. and I can clearly see the view.. I feel safe.. as I think about moving **up** these well-lit stairs.. I feel warm as I think about climbing **up** this stunning staircase..

as I take in the view.. I have a sense of anticipation.. as I am looking forward to moving further **up** the staircase.. I feel totally safe, perfectly secure.. as I continue to climb **up** the steps.. I momentarily pause.. taking in a **deep** breath…. I look out of the window and I see the rooftops.. they look like dolls houses.. they are fun and interesting from this view..

from this moment.. as I continue to climb **up**.. I decide to count from one to five… when I reach **five**.. I know I will be perfectly relaxed, and in my own natural state of peace and perfect relaxation.. counting **up now**..

every time I read the **words in bold**.. and with every suggestion I give myself, **will** sink in **so deeply** into the unconscious part of my mind, **now**..

One.. feeling good.. feeling fine.. gently at peace.. fully at ease.. totally safe and perfectly secure.. as I continue to focus on my breath…. I feel myself surrendering to the deep and perfect relaxation that is filling my body.. **now**..

I feel **fine**.. totally safe and perfectly secure.. moving **up**.. and yet going into a **deeper** sense of **relaxation**.. every time I say a number out loud.. it causes me to go **deeper** and **deeper** into **relaxation**..

Two.. as I continue to move *up* the stairs, I pause to look out of the window again.. taking in a *deep* breath…. *now*, I see and view the tops of the trees.. they look magnificent..

from this moment, as I continue to climb *up*.. I become more and more curious.. I feel myself becoming *more* and *more relaxed*.. gently at peace.. feeling good.. totally safe.. perfectly secure.. moving *up*, yet, going into a *deeper* sense of *relaxation*.. every time I say a number out loud.. it causes me to go deeper and deeper into *relaxation*..

Three.. feeling good, feeling fine.. totally safe.. perfectly secure.. as I continue to focus on my breath…. *now*, I feel myself surrendering to the deep and perfect relaxation that is filling my body.. I feel fine.. totally safe, perfectly secure.. moving *up* the stairs, yet going into a *deeper* sense of *relaxation*.. as I continue to read out loud.. every time I say a number.. it causes me to go even more deeper and *deeper* into **relaxation**.. feeling gently at peace, feeling good.. feeling fine, totally safe.. and perfectly secure..

Four.. feeling good, feeling fine.. and gently at peace.. fully at *ease*.. totally safe and perfectly secure.. as I continue to **breathe deeply**…. I feel myself surrendering to the deep and perfect relaxation, *now*.. filling my body..

as I continue to move *up* the stairs.. I pause to look out of the window again.. taking in a *deep* breath…. I am *now* in awe of the mountain peaks.. I see them glistening from the rays of the sun coming through the clouds.. they look majestic.. and they look glorious..

from this moment.. as I continue to climb *up*.. I become more and more curious as to where this is taking me.. and feel myself

215

more and *more relaxed*.. gently at peace.. feeling good.. totally safe.. perfectly secure.. moving *up*, yet going into a deeper sense of relaxation.. every time I say a number out loud.. it causes me to go *deeper* and *deeper* into *relaxation*..

Five.. feeling wonder-struck and totally safe.. perfectly secure.. I take a *deep* breath.... as I have surrendered *now* to the deep and perfect *relaxation* that has *now* filled my body.. I feel fine.. totally safe and perfectly secure..

I reach the top of the staircase.. and see a warden guarding a beautiful archway.. the warden gives me a protective nod.. and I realize that it is *me* who is architect of this stunning staircase.. and it is *me* who has stationed the warden here .. for my protection..

feeling safe and perfectly secure.. I *easily* bypass the warden.. I *easily* walk out onto the balcony.. and find myself gently being in the most comfortable position.. feeling a perfect state of *relaxation*.

as I relax and focus on my breath.... I *now* find myself sitting above the clouds.. I feel completely at *ease* and I begin to feel a *beautiful sensation* of peace and relaxation, tranquility and calm.. I imagine the *ideal me* projected onto the sky like a movie screen *now*.. as I picture myself, my mind and body feels a wonderful *sense of calm*, and feels gently at peace..

I made a *good decision* to climb the staircase, as I can *now* see myself more clearly, and with a better view.. I see myself as I am.. *I Am so relaxed*.. that my mind has become so sensitive.. so receptive to what I read out loud.. that every time I read the *words in bold*.. and with every suggestion I give myself, *will* sink in *so deeply* into the unconscious part of my mind.. that it will begin to cause such a *lasting impression* there, *now*..

tranquility and calm are flowing through my mind and body like a cool breeze, giving me such a pleasant feeling.. such a beautiful sensation... as I embed positive suggestions into my unconscious mind, I *now* acknowledge *my true value*.. these suggestions exercise a greater and *greater influence* to the way I think.. over the way I feel.. over the way I behave.. and the way *I become smartyr*.

every time I read the *words in bold*.. and with every suggestion *I give myself,* will sink in so deeply.. into the unconscious part of my mind.. that it will begin to cause such a *lasting impression, now*.. and *will* remain firmly embedded in the unconscious part of my mind, *now*.. even after I have stopped reading out loud..

I feel good that *I am* interested in improving my life.. and.. just *now*.. *I am* finding ways to develop my smartyr Self.. and I *now*.. know putting empathy into action is an art *worth practicing*.. and that the expression of my compassion exhibits my empathy into action.. *now*.. as *my empathy matures*, I provide support for myself and for others.. I refuse investing in feeling better, because *now, I am invested in getting better at feeling*..

now.. drifting deeper and deeper all the time as I continue to listen to my voice.. I *hear my voice*, I slow down, I drift deeper and deeper.. I feel a wonderful sense of calm..

my smartyr self knows the difference between sympathy with empathy.. I know that being sympathetic means that I can think and feel *for* another.. and being empathic *now* means that *I can feel with another*..

my compassion challenges my assumptions.. and I like that, because it keeps me humble.. and *my heart opens*.. I know my compassion is the greatest of virtues, aspired in me as the noblest quality of my heart..

my compassion is contagious, so *I lead by example*.. I do not treat people as bad as they are.. I treat them *as good as I am*.. *now,* my empathy drives me to understand the perspectives, the needs, and the intentions of others..

my compassion and *my curiosity* influences me *now*.. to suspend judgment towards myself and others.. my empathic responses benefit from *my patience*.. *my willpower*.. and *my deliberate discipline*..

now.. I do not fall out of love.. I fall out of tolerance.. *I am mindful* of how much I tolerate.. as *I am aware* I am teaching others how to treat me *now*.. and *I am prepared*.. and *I am skilled* to deal with the monsters in my head *now*.. rather than push negative emotions I am experiencing, onto and into others.. as a smartyr, I can accept failings and weaknesses.. in my myself and in other..

I am sensitive, *I am perceptive* and *I am appropriate*.. I can maintain a distinction between myself and another *now*.. as I express deeply from my own felt sense.. my empathy leads me to create close friendships, long-lasting relationships.. and caring communities..

these suggestions will continue to influence and become part of my natural inner dialogue as I go about my day.. every day I will become so deeply interested in whatever *I am doing*.. whatever *I am feeling*.. whatever *I am thinking*.. and whatever is going on around me.. that my mind will be in a state of relaxation..

I am.. going to *feel physically stronger* and.. I will *feel more alert*.. more wide awake.. *more energetic*.. and much less easily discouraged..

I will wake up from my self-hypnotic trance by counting to three.. while reading out-loud.. when I get to number *three*.. I will be wide awake, fully alert, and will be *feeling better than ever before*..

Three.. feeling *satisfied* and *proud*, I am beginning to awaken from my hypnotic trance..

Two. becoming aware of my body, *I am excited* about the positive results from this session..

ONE, ONE, ONE, now, wide awake, refreshed and *feeling better than ever before!*

Post Hypnosis Reflections

* Check-out with how you feel using the following list. Mentally scan your body and tick the boxes that best describe how you feel
* Your results will vary depending on your regularity and repetition on completing the series
* Journal any thoughts, feelings or insights that may emerge on the following pages
* Notice, observe and feel into the subtle shifts in your daily interactions as this is the trajectory for preferrable life changes to eventually occur

Post Self-hypnosis
Check-out

Negative	Despair	Angry	Insignificant
Resentful	Low	Frustrated	Suspicious
Critical	Guilty	Disapproving	Miserable
Neutral	Confused	Inquisitive	Vulnerable
Relieved	Excited	Amazed	Interested
Furious	Hopeless	Disappointed	Powerful
Stuck	Determined	Trapped	Blocked
Bitter	Unhappy	Impressed	Disgruntled
Alive	Let Down	Irritated	Anxious
Joyful	Nervous	Annoyed	Insecure
Resistant	Hesitant	Happy	Weak
Bored	Cautious	Powerless	Rejected
Content	Hopeful	Grief	Embarrassed
Curious	Inspired	Victimised	Fearful
Awful	Neglected	Optimistic	Surprised
Scared	Overwhelmed	Lonely	Creative
Inadequate	Helpless	Energetic	Heartbroken
Tense	Calm	Tired	Hesitant
Eager	Worried	Hurt	Safe
Restless	Apprehensive	Regretful	Grateful
Unsure	Judgemental	Confident	Valued
Shocked	Worthless	Thankful	Abandoned
Playful	Glad	Depressed	Withdrawn

Journaling
Insights - Thoughts - Reflections

Journaling
Insights - Thoughts - Reflections

Developing Smartyr Social Skills

Chapter 24

Developing Smartyr Social Skills

Developing social skills is a universal characteristic that is governed by culture, collective beliefs, and attitudes. They continuously change and evolve throughout our lives. Social skills adapt to different societies' customs and values as we now communicate and interact globally. Social skills development is an integral part of functioning and is linked to early childhood development. We all yearn to be wanted and need to have a sense of belonging. Feeling valued is crucial for healthy self-worth and self-esteem and adds value to society, which is the very fabric of civilization.

Suppose you are to create a new kind of revolution in the way you live, you not only need to discover who you are through self-reflection, but you also need to become interested and curious in the lives of others. Smartyrs have learned how to get along with others and manage relationships. For the developing smartyr, mastering good social skills will provide you with a foundation for a lifetime of healthier relationships in all aspects of your life.

You are not born with social skills, they are initially cultivated and learned during your childhood through interaction with your significant caregivers and play with peers. However, the process can be disrupted if you have suffered from neglect or have other developmental or learning difficulties. Especially if there is a diagnosis on the Autistic spectrum, and as a result, you are more likely to face significant communication, social, and behavioral challenges. Autism spectrum disorder or not, most of us, unfortunately, experience social failure at various stages during childhood, which interferes with the ability to learn and arrests our developing self-esteem.

If parents have poor or low functioning social skills, failure is inevitably experienced by the child despite their best intentions. If left undeveloped and not knowing how best to cultivate social skills, you can feel socially isolated and lonely. Depression and damaged self-esteem ensue, along with experiencing anger, frustration, and conflicting relationships.

You can unlearn poor social behaviors when choosing to foster the currency for better quality relationships and social acceptability. You must first cultivate and nurture greater awareness towards your own inner dialogue; what do you say to yourself when no-one else is listening? And secondly, by developing your active listening skills and knowing how best to use them. These skills give you the ability to tune into the sensitivity of reading and responding to another's cues and nuances. When you want to flourish into your smartyr Self, it is worth exercising your social skills!

Cultivating social skills is perhaps the most critical set of abilities a smartyr can have. Consideration towards others, having good manners and communicating effectively, and expressing needs is the foundation for solid social skills. In adulthood, emotionally relating to others in healthy ways is tantamount to harmonious relationships, effective leadership, and teamwork. In general, relationships are happier, resilient, and emotionally satisfying.

As a smartyr, you become socially competent and instinctively understand the dance of relatedness. Social data is processed, and behavioral responses are readily available to help you navigate your social arena. Life-affirming social skills promote influential and inspirational flair. As a smartyr, you add value and become aspirational to others which develops your character and charisma and evolves you into the kind of person other people want to be around. Others may forget what you have said, but they will never forget how you left them feeling.

Improving your relationships with others supports you in having good mental health. Having close friendships or participating in social networks can help you take care of your own needs while being respectful and considerate of others' needs. Having close relationships will help lower your stress and anxiety levels and generally lift your mood as you feel more supported and less lonely.

It is never too late to develop your social skills as we are ever evolving and growing. Cultivating and practicing communication skills is also about exploring non-verbal communication, mastering conversation skills, appreciating the benefit of small talk, and sharpening your assertiveness abilities.

When you learn to accept your feelings and how your emotions affect your body, you can be confident and have greater mastery in controlling how you present yourself in social settings. You will be able to differentiate your feelings from another person. Therefore, feel much more comfortable accepting other people's feelings and emotions and managing the interaction with greater clarity.

Considerations

To create a more profound interaction, use words that people resonate with. Mixing styles when interacting can appeal to people's different senses and make the connection more exciting and memorable.

If you observe the nuances of people, their preferred method of communication will become evident. Learning to match and mirror them will help build rapport. It is beneficial to recognize your primary mode of communication in the following three different styles of communicating:

* **Visual** – they tend to look up and to the side as they process information and use statements such as: 'Let's see…, I imagine…, I can't quite picture it.'
* **Sound-related** (Auditory) – will primarily move their eyes left to right or right to left as they 'need' to hear the information and use statements such as: 'That sounds about right…, That rings a bell…, That's music to my ears.'
* **Feeling/touch-based** (Kinaesthetic) – will primarily look down and to the right as they 'need' to feel the information and use statements such as: 'That feels right…, Stay in touch…, 'I have a good feeling about.'

As a smartyr, you behave like a social person. You make a deliberate effort to improve your social skills and have not allowed fear and anxiety to stop you from being curious about people and entering conversations.

You will recognize the benefits of small talk as a conversation about things that are not of great importance. Adopting open body language along with light, casual conversation lets the other person know you are approachable, friendly, and interested. The real value and purpose of small talk is to create rapport leading to a deeper, trusting and more meaningful interaction and communication.

* Key components of open body language a smartyr adopts are smiling, maintaining eye contact, nodding, relaxing your shoulders, turning towards the other, standing or sitting up straight, and uncrossing your legs and arms.

* People are better at small talk when they become better listeners, so encourage others to talk while you listen and settle into the interaction; being quiet allows you to take in what the other is saying. This will also give you time to get comfortable, feel less awkward and self-conscious.

* Reveal or share something about yourself, such as 'It was nice to catch the bus here today as I usually drive.'

* Become familiar with using open-ended questions. The other person will know that you are receptive and willing to communicate. A closed question forces a yes or no answer, such as, 'Do you like living here?' An opened-ended question supports a person to elaborate. For example, 'What do you think about living here?' or 'How do you feel about living here?'

* Notice when conversations turn lukewarm to cold. Practice noticing social cues and when to naturally begin to end a conversation.

* Practice staying present, attentive, and attuned to another because people like talking about themselves

and build on what they say with related thoughts and questions.

* Consciously listen to facts and feelings that another may share with you and highlight commonalities. It is part of our nature to search for the common ground so that we can feel connected to the person we are with.

* Offer observations, insights, and compliments, follow it up with a question and let the conversation flow naturally.

Developing social skills results in immediate benefits. These can include feeling better about yourself, liking who you are, being accepted more socially, and having fewer confrontations and better quality relationships; you learn to manage disagreements in a more adult way.

Journaling
Insights - Thoughts - Reflections

Develop your Character
&
Charisma
✵
Smartyr
Self-hypnosis

How to Read the Smartyr Script Out Loud

* We recommend the minimum requirement to complete the series is to read one smartyr script each day in the same sequence for six weeks. This method works more powerfully when used regularly and with commitment

* Before you start, check-in with how you feel using the following list. Mentally scan your body and tick the boxes that best describe how you feel

* Read the script right through from start to finish, it is important you take your time because each hypnosis is purposefully repetitive which adds to the powerful relaxation and trance-like state which is needed for hypnosis

* Start reading aloud in a slow, calm, and purposeful assertive tone

* Pronounce each word fully so it feels like the message you want to convey

* Pause and take a breath where indicated by the dots within the script

* If using a metronome, set it at 50, and allow two full beats before continuing to read

* Read-aloud words written in bold, extended, and italics with emphasis and conviction

* When you finish, check-out with how you feel. Mentally scan your body and tick the boxes that best describe how you feel, compare with your check-in

* Use the journaling pages at the end of each hypnosis to support your progress, insights, thoughts, and reflections

Pre Self-hypnosis
Check-in

Negative	Despair	Angry	Insignificant
Resentful	Low	Frustrated	Suspicious
Critical	Guilty	Disapproving	Miserable
Neutral	Confused	Inquisitive	Vulnerable
Relieved	Excited	Amazed	Interested
Furious	Hopeless	Disappointed	Powerful
Stuck	Determined	Trapped	Blocked
Bitter	Unhappy	Impressed	Disgruntled
Alive	Let Down	Irritated	Anxious
Joyful	Nervous	Annoyed	Insecure
Resistant	Hesitant	Happy	Weak
Bored	Cautious	Powerless	Rejected
Content	Hopeful	Grief	Embarrassed
Curious	Inspired	Victimised	Fearful
Awful	Neglected	Optimistic	Surprised
Scared	Overwhelmed	Lonely	Creative
Inadequate	Helpless	Energetic	Heartbroken
Tense	Calm	Tired	Hesitant
Eager	Worried	Hurt	Safe
Restless	Apprehensive	Regretful	Grateful
Unsure	Judgemental	Confident	Valued
Shocked	Worthless	Thankful	Abandoned
Playful	Glad	Depressed	Withdrawn

Develop Your Character & Charisma
Smartyr Self-Hypnosis

every time I read the ***words in bold..*** and with every suggestion I give myself, ***will*** sink in ***so deeply*** into the unconscious part of my mind, ***now..*** feeling settled and taking in a deep breath.... I continue to focus on my breath.. I allow my body to become more settled and more relaxed.. I feel a tingling on the top of my head.. as I continue to become more and more relaxed.. I feel gently at peace.. fully at ease.. totally safe.. and perfectly secure and comfortable..

as my relaxation ***deepens, now..*** I feel a wonderful sense of calmness traveling down the back of my head.. I have a sense of warmth and sense of tingling and I have become ***more*** and ***more relaxed..*** I welcome this gentle and warm relaxation filling my body, ***now..***

as I read out loud.. I can feel this sense of relaxation moving the down the front of my face.. and I feel the tiny muscles around my eyes relaxing.. my mouth relaxing.. and my jaw relaxing.. to the soothing and calming tone of my voice..

my breath is in tune with my heartbeat, making me feel a ***deeper*** sense of ***relaxation..*** this wonderful sense of ***calm..*** and peace moves down my neck and relaxes my shoulders and my chest.. as I continue to read out loud the soothing sound of my voice relaxes the rest of my body.. right to the soles of my feet.. tingling and becoming perfectly ***relaxed..*** as I continue to focus on my breath.... becoming more and more ***relaxed..***

every time I read the ***words in bold..*** and with every suggestion I give myself, ***will*** sink in ***so deeply*** into the unconscious part of my mind, **now**.. I see myself moving toward a wide set of well-lit stairs.. I approach this beautiful staircase.. and I am curious where it leads me.. I am surrounded by large protective panes of glass.. and I can clearly see the view.. I feel safe.. as I think about moving **up** these well-lit stairs.. I feel warm as I think about climbing **up** this stunning staircase..

as I take in the view.. I have a sense of anticipation.. as I am looking forward to moving further **up** the staircase.. I feel totally safe, perfectly secure.. as I continue to climb **up** the steps.. I momentarily pause.. taking in a **deep** breath.... I look out of the window and I see the rooftops.. they look like dolls houses.. they are fun and interesting from this view..

from this moment.. as I continue to climb **up**.. I decide to count from one to five... when I reach **five**.. I know I will be perfectly relaxed, and in my own natural state of peace and perfect relaxation.. counting **up now**..

every time I read the **words in bold**.. and with every suggestion I give myself, **will** sink in **so deeply** into the unconscious part of my mind, **now**..

One.. feeling good.. feeling fine.. gently at peace.. fully at ease.. totally safe and perfectly secure.. as I continue to focus on my breath.... I feel myself surrendering to the deep and perfect relaxation that is filling my body.. **now**..

I feel **fine**.. totally safe and perfectly secure.. moving **up**.. and yet going into a **deeper** sense of **relaxation**.. every time I say a number out loud.. it causes me to go **deeper** and **deeper** into **relaxation**..

Two.. as I continue to move **up** the stairs, I pause to look out of the window again.. taking in a **deep** breath…. **now**, I see and view the tops of the trees.. they look magnificent..

from this moment, as I continue to climb **up**.. I become more and more curious.. I feel myself becoming **more** and **more** **relaxed**.. gently at peace.. feeling good.. totally safe.. perfectly secure.. moving **up**, yet, going into a **deeper** sense of **relaxation**.. every time I say a number out loud.. it causes me to go deeper and deeper into **relaxation**..

Three.. feeling good, feeling fine.. totally safe.. perfectly secure.. as I continue to focus on my breath…. **now**, I feel myself surrendering to the deep and perfect relaxation that is filling my body.. I feel fine.. totally safe, perfectly secure.. moving **up** the stairs, yet going into a **deeper** sense of **relaxation**.. as I continue to read out loud.. every time I say a number.. it causes me to go even more deeper and **deeper** into **relaxation**.. feeling gently at peace, feeling good.. feeling fine, totally safe.. and perfectly secure..

Four.. feeling good, feeling fine.. and gently at peace.. fully at **ease**.. totally safe and perfectly secure.. as I continue to **breathe** **deeply**…. I feel myself surrendering to the deep and perfect relaxation, **now**.. filling my body..

as I continue to move **up** the stairs.. I pause to look out of the window again.. taking in a **deep** breath…. I am **now** in awe of the mountain peaks.. I see them glistening from the rays of the sun coming through the clouds.. they look majestic.. and they look glorious..

from this moment.. as I continue to climb *up*.. I become more and more curious as to where this is taking me.. and feel myself *more* and *more relaxed*.. gently at peace.. feeling good.. totally safe.. perfectly secure.. moving *up*, yet going into a deeper sense of relaxation.. every time I say a number out loud.. it causes me to go *deeper* and *deeper* into *relaxation*..

Five.. feeling wonder-struck and totally safe.. perfectly secure.. I take a *deep* breath.... as I have surrendered *now* to the deep and perfect *relaxation* that has *now* filled my body.. I feel fine.. totally safe and perfectly secure..

I reach the top of the staircase.. and see a warden guarding a beautiful archway.. the warden gives me a protective nod.. and I realize that it is *me* who is architect of this stunning staircase.. and it is *me* who has stationed the warden here .. for my protection..

feeling safe and perfectly secure.. I *easily* bypass the warden.. I *easily* walk out onto the balcony.. and find myself gently being in the most comfortable position.. feeling a perfect state of *relaxation*.

as I relax and focus on my breath.... I *now* find myself sitting above the clouds.. I feel completely at *ease* and I begin to feel a *beautiful sensation* of peace and relaxation, tranquility and calm.. I imagine the *ideal me* projected onto the sky like a movie screen *now*.. as I picture myself, my mind and body feels a wonderful *sense of calm*, and feels gently at peace..

I made a *good decision* to climb the staircase, as I can *now* see myself more clearly, and with a better view.. I see myself as I am.. *I Am so relaxed*.. that my mind has become so sensitive..

so receptive to what I read out loud.. that every time I read the **words in bold**.. and with every suggestion I give myself, **will** sink in **so deeply** into the unconscious part of my mind.. that it will begin to cause such a **lasting impression** there, **now**..

tranquility and calm are flowing through my mind and body like a cool breeze, giving me such a pleasant feeling.. such a beautiful sensation... as I embed positive suggestions into my unconscious mind, I **now** acknowledge **my true value**.. these suggestions exercise a greater and **greater influence** to the way I think.. over the way I feel.. over the way I behave.. and the way **I become smartyr.**

every time I read the **words in bold**.. and with every suggestion **I give myself,** will sink in so deeply.. into the unconscious part of my mind.. that it will begin to cause such a **lasting impression,** **now**.. and **will** remain firmly embedded in the unconscious part of my mind, **now**.. even after I have stopped reading out loud..

I feel good that **I am** interested in improving my life.. and.. just **now**.. **I am** finding ways to develop my smartyr self.. I am **now**.. curious to discover who I am thorough self-reflection.. I continually hone my social skills as I know this helps me to develop my character.. **I have a genuine spark** of life that rubs off on others.. being charismatic, **now, I exude joy** and enthusiasm about life..

now.. drifting deeper and deeper all the time as I continue to listen to my voice.. I **hear my voice**, I slow down, I drift deeper and deeper.. I feel a wonderful sense of calm..

now.. **I feel good**.. my self-worth and self-esteem is heightened.. my passion and my conviction oozes out of me.. it gives me a *sense of value*.. I am interested and curious in the lives of others.. it gives me a *sense of belonging, now*..

as a smartyr, cultivating social skills is the most critical set of abilities I can have.. *I am inspirational, now*.. *I am aspirational* .. and others appreciate my authenticity and my company.. I can *deeply connect*, I can *attract*, I can *influence* the currency for better quality relationships and social acceptability..

I can *emotionally relate* to others in healthy ways, *now*.. because I know, to instinctively understand the dance of relatedness, is tantamount to me being socially skilled.. I know how to match and mirror others, because I know how to build rapport.. *I am considerate, now*.. and, *I have good manners*..

I can adopt open body language.. entering into conversations is *easy, now*.. because I have learned the benefits of small talk.... I am able to have light, casual conversations.. and others feel *I am approachable*, friendly and interested in them, *now*..

my *smartyr character* and my *smartyr charisma* has allowed me to *grow my edges* and to become the kind of person people want to be around, *now*.. I know that others may forget what I have said, but they will *always* remember how I leave them feeling..

these suggestions will continue to influence and become part of my natural inner dialogue as I go about my day.. every day I will become so deeply interested in whatever *I am doing*.. whatever *I am feeling*.. whatever *I am thinking*.. and whatever is going on around me.. that my mind will be in a state of relaxation..

I am.. going to *feel physically stronger* and.. I will *feel more alert..* more wide awake.. *more energetic..* and much less easily discouraged..

I will wake up from my self-hypnotic trance by counting to three.. while reading out-loud.. when I get to number *three..* I will be wide awake, fully alert, and will be *feeling better than ever before..*

Three.. feeling *satisfied* and *proud*, I am beginning to awaken from my hypnotic trance..

Two. Becoming aware of my body, *I am excited* about the positive results from this session..

ONE, ONE, ONE, now, wide awake, refreshed and *feeling better than ever before!*

Post Hypnosis Reflections

* Check-out with how you feel using the following list. Mentally scan your body and tick the boxes that best describe how you feel
* Your results will vary depending on your regularity and repetition on completing the series
* Journal any thoughts, feelings or insights that may emerge on the following pages
* Notice, observe and feel into the subtle shifts in your daily interactions as this is the trajectory for preferable life changes to eventually occur

Post Self-hypnosis
Check-out

Negative	Despair	Angry	Insignificant
Resentful	Low	Frustrated	Suspicious
Critical	Guilty	Disapproving	Miserable
Neutral	Confused	Inquisitive	Vulnerable
Relieved	Excited	Amazed	Interested
Furious	Hopeless	Disappointed	Powerful
Stuck	Determined	Trapped	Blocked
Bitter	Unhappy	Impressed	Disgruntled
Alive	Let Down	Irritated	Anxious
Joyful	Nervous	Annoyed	Insecure
Resistant	Hesitant	Happy	Weak
Bored	Cautious	Powerless	Rejected
Content	Hopeful	Grief	Embarrassed
Curious	Inspired	Victimised	Fearful
Awful	Neglected	Optimistic	Surprised
Scared	Overwhelmed	Lonely	Creative
Inadequate	Helpless	Energetic	Heartbroken
Tense	Calm	Tired	Hesitant
Eager	Worried	Hurt	Safe
Restless	Apprehensive	Regretful	Grateful
Unsure	Judgemental	Confident	Valued
Shocked	Worthless	Thankful	Abandoned
Playful	Glad	Depressed	Withdrawn

Journaling
Insights - Thoughts - Reflections

Journaling
Insights - Thoughts - Reflections

A Personal Message
from the Authors

There will be many signs as you progress towards smartyrdom. We want to thank you for reading this book. It has been a labor of love yet a source of absolute pleasure as we have thought about you and the limitlessness of your mind and spirit, and how you will use the information provided in this book to improve your life and create a life of your dreams.

Cultivating compassion will help you during times when you may feel bored, resistant, or restless. Compassion aspires you to remain tolerant, accept your failings and honor painful discoveries. Humility gives you the purpose to re-evaluate your prejudices and any self-judgments. Having the right attitude will help with any internal conflicts that may arise, forcing premature outcomes and accepting moments of hesitation.

Believe today that you can be better than yesterday, and you will witness results when you take action on this belief. As you go back into your ordinary lives, continue to witness life experiences, lead a triumphant life, and manifest being smartyr in every atom of your body. We know what we want for you. Our desire for you is clear-cut and definite. We know that you possess the power to become smartyr, learn how to draw upon it, and become aspiring to others.

We offer you heartfelt blessings and compassion, and through this book, we walk with you on your journey to smartyrdom.

THE END

Continue to Enjoy the Journey

Appendix A

List of Personal Values

Ability	Anticipation	Bravery
Abundance	Appreciation	Brilliance
Acceptance	Approachability	Briskness
Accessibility	Artfulness	Calmness
Accessibility	Assertiveness	Camaraderie
Accomplishment	Assurance	Candor
Accountability	Attention to detail	Capability
Accuracy	Attentiveness	Care
Achievement	Attractiveness	Career
Activity	Audacity	Carefulness
Adaptability	Authenticity	Caring
Advancement	Authority	Certainty
Adventure	Autonomy	Challenge
Advocacy	Availability	Change
Affection	Balance	Character
Affective	Being the best	Charisma
Affluence	Being-ness	Charity
Aggressive	Belonging	Charm
Agility	Benevolence	Chastity
Alertness	Best people	Cheerfulness
Altruism	Blissfulness	Citizenship
Amusement	Boldness	Clarity
Anti-corporate	Buoyancy	Classy

Clear-minded	Connection	Depth
Cleverness	Consciousness	Desire
Clients	Contentment	Determination
Closeness	Continuity	Development
Cognizance	Contribution	Devotion
Collaboration	Control	Devoutness
Comfort	Conviction	Dexterity
Commitment	Conviviality	Different
Common sense	Coolness	Differentiation
Commonality	Cooperation	Dignity
Communication	Coordination	Diligence
Community	Copiousness	Diplomacy
Compassion	Cordiality	Direct
Competency	Correctness	Direction
Completion	Courage	Directness
Composure	Courtesy	Discipline
Comprehensive	Craftiness	Discovery
Concentration	Craftsmanship	Diversity
Concern for others	Deference	Dominance
Confidence	Delicacy	Down-to-earth
Confidentiality	Delight	Dreaming
Conformity	Democratic	Drive
Congruency	Dependability	Duty

Dynamism	Equitable	Family atmosphere
Eagerness	Ethics	Famous
Ease of use	Evolution	Fascination
Economy	Exactness	Fashion
Ecstasy	Equitable	Fearlessness
Education	Excellence	Feelings
Effectiveness	Excitement	Ferocious
Efficiency	Exhilaration	Fidelity
Elation	Expectancy	Fierce
Elegance	Expediency	Finances
Empathy	Experience	Finesse
Empowerment	Expertise	Firmness
Encouragement	Exploration	Fitness
Endurance	Expression	Flair
Energy	Extravagance	Flexibility
Engagement	Extroversion	Flow
Enjoyment	Exuberance	Fluency
Enlightenment	Facilitation	Fluidity
Entertainment	Fairness	Focus
Enthusiasm	Faith	Foresight
Entrepreneurship	Faithfulness	Forgiveness
Environment	Fame	Formal
Equality	Family	Fortitude

Frankness	Guidance	Impious
Freedom	Happiness	Improvement
Fresh ideas	Hard work	Inclusiveness
Friendliness	Harmony	Independence
Friendship	Health	Individuality
Friendships	Heart	Industry
Frugality	Helpfulness	Influence
Fun	Heroism	Informal
Fun-loving	Holiness	Ingenuity
Gallantry	Home	Inner harmony
Generosity	Honesty	Innovation
Genius	Honor	Innovative
Gentility	Hope	Inquisitiveness
Genuineness	Hopefulness	Insightfulness
Giving	Hospitality	Inspiration
Goodness	Humanity	Instinctiveness
Goodwill	Humility	Integrity
Grace	Humor	Intelligence
Gratefulness	Hygiene	Intensity
Gratitude	Imagination	Intimacy
Greatness	Impact	Intrepidness
Gregarious	Impartiality	Introversion
Growth	Impeccability	Intuition

Intuitiveness	Maximizing	Persistence
Inventiveness	Meaning	Personal development
Investment	Moderation	Playfulness
Inviting	Mysteriousness	Pleasantness
Involvement	Mystery	Pleasure
Irreverence	Neatness	Plentiful-ness
Lavishness	Obedience	Poise
Lawful	Open-mindedness	Popularity
Leadership	Optimism	Positivity
Learning	Opulence	Potency
Level-headed	Outlandishness	Potential
Liberation	Outrageousness	Power
Liberty	Partnership	Powerfulness
Listening	Passion	Pre-eminence
Liveliness	Patience	Precision
Lively	Patriotism	Preparedness
Logic	Peace	Presence
Longevity	Peacefulness	Preservation
Love	People	Pride
Love of career	Perceptiveness	Privacy
Loyalty	Perfection	Proactivity
Majesty	Performance	Productivity
Maturity	Perseverance	Professionalism

Proficiency	Resilience	Saintliness
Profitability	Resolution	Sanguinity
Progress	Resolve	Sanitary
Prudence	Resourcefulness	Satisfaction
Punctuality	Respect	Security
Purity	Respect for me	Self-awareness
Purpose	Respect for others	Self-control
Rational	Responsibility	Self-directed
Readiness	Responsiveness	Self-motivation
Realism	Rest	Self-realization
Realistic	Restfulness	Self-reliance
Reason	Restraint	Self-respect
Reciprocity	Results	Self-responsibility
Recognition	Results-oriented	Selfless
Recreation	Reverence	Selflessness
Refinement	Richness	Sense of humor
Reflection	Rigor	Sensitivity
Relationships	Risk taking	Sensuality
Relaxation	Rule of law	Serenity
Reliability	Sacredness	Serious
Religion	Sacrifice	Service
Renewal	Safety	Sexuality
Reputation	Sagacity	Shared prosperity

Sharing	Stealth	Truth
Shrewdness	Stewardship	Understanding
Significance	Stillness	Unflappable
Silence	Strength	Uniqueness
Silliness	Structure	Unity
Simplicity	Substantiality	Universal
Sincerity	Success	Usefulness
Skillfulness	Sufficiency	Utility
Skill	Support	Valor
Smartness	Thoroughness	Value
Solidarity	Thoughtfulness	Value creation
Solidity	Thrift	Variety
Solitude	Timeliness	Versatility
Sophistication	Tolerance	Victorious
Soundness	Toughness	Vigor
Speed	Traditional	Virtue
Spirit	Training	Vision
Spiritualism	Tranquility	Vitality
Spirituality	Transcendence	Vivacity
Spontaneity	Transparency	Warmth
Stability	Trust	Watchfulness
Standardization	Trusting your gut	Wealth
Status	Trustworthiness	Welcoming

Well-being
Wellness
Wholesomeness
Willfulness
Will
Willingness
Wisdom
Wittiness
Wonder
Work/life balance
Worthiness
Zeal
Zest
Zing

Appendix B

Frequently Asked Questions

How many times should I practice each of the read-aloud smartyr self-hypnosis?

The minimum requirement is once a day for 20 minutes, but if time affords you, practice as much as you want. The more you practice, the more proficient you will become.

✷

How many sessions of each read-aloud smartyr self-hypnosis do you recommend?

We recommend the minimum requirement to complete the series is to read one smartyr script each day in the same sequence for six weeks. For example, Monday: I Am. Tuesday: Connect thoughts with feelings. Wednesday: Awakening your smartyr self. Thursday: Intrinsic motivation. Friday: Cultivate empathy and compassion. Saturday: Developing your character and charisma. Once the series is complete, feel free to read any of them at any time and as much as you like depending on your time and availability.

✷

Is there a good time of day to practice self-hypnosis?

The best time to practice is early morning or last thing at night. However, you can practice any time of day if you can find a quiet and private pocket of time.

What can I do if I don't feel the hypnotic state during my session?

At first, you may not feel the hypnotic state, but you will experience a state of relaxation. Make sure you complete the pre and post-hypnosis check-in list, as this will help you evaluate the subtle differences immediately before and after each session. When reading the smartyr self-hypnosis regularly, you will notice the impact of your reading intensifies, and feelings stir while reading elements of the script. This indicates that you are reaching a deeper trance–like state and your skill is improving, and change is happening. Remember, hypnosis is a very natural state, and we enter this state many times without even noticing. Any activity with a concentrated engagement can drift us into a natural auto-pilot mode, and this includes reading.

How soon before I notice changes in my life?

This depends on the regularity of your practice and your firm intentions and motivation. The more you practice, the more likely things will change. However, we suggest you pay attention to the subtle changes in your life. These subtle changes are indicators that things are happening, and you are becoming more proficient at self-hypnosis. Journaling your insights, thoughts, and reflections at the end of each script will help you notice the changes happening around you and help you generate any evidence of change.

✳

What do I do if I don't experience results after multiple repetitions of practice?

If you do not experience any results after multiple repetitions of practice, make sure you are honest about the changes you sincerely want to make; are you ready to move out of martyrdom? To become smartyr, you will need the firm belief that self-hypnosis works along with the expectation that you will succeed. You want to have a clear path so you can appraise who you are and who you want to be, so remind yourself why you are doing it.

✳

Can I use this book at the same time as seeing a professional therapist?

Yes. This book is an excellent companion guide for your personal development. Using the pre and post-check-in lists and the journaling pages of insights, thoughts and reflections will allow you the opportunity for deeper exploration in your therapy sessions.

✳

Can I record the hypnosis in my own voice and then playback the recording?

Yes. What a good idea! However, our read–aloud smartyr self-hypnosis is designed to combine your voice with conscious visual scanning of the page. This helps the hypnotic trance become effective so that you absorb the therapeutic autosuggestions directly into your subconscious mind. However, you can record your voice and play it back like a guided meditation. Ideally, do this first thing in the morning, just before you are fully awake or just before you go to sleep. This is an excellent way to reinforce and further embed the positive messages.

✳

I am feeling anxious about the hypnosis – will I be able to 'snap out of it' if need to?

You have the ability to snap out of any trance-like state at any given moment and at any time. Be assured you will be able to automatically and immediately emerge out of your hypnotic trance and be fully awake, alert, and be able to attend to any emergency that may require your attention. It is rare to experience problematic effects from self-hypnosis. Still, we advise that if you experience sudden anxiety or are struggling with anxiety before you begin, we recommend that you postpone self-hypnosis practice and seek medical advice first. Remember, all deliberate hypnosis is effectively a form of self-hypnosis which means the control is always with you.

Can I use the read-aloud smartyr self-hypnosis to another person and hypnotize them?

Why not! Experiment. The least they will get is into a state of relaxation. Remember, the control will always be with them, and they will decide on the effectiveness of the words you read to them.

Acknowledgments

Shaun Brookhouse is an Honorary Fellow of UKCP and a practitioner of hypnosis since 1989 and a trainer of therapists since 1993. He is the past principal of the National College of Hypnosis and Psychotherapy and is the Director of Brookhouse Hypnotherapy Ltd, a Manchester-based Hypno-Psychotherapy practice. He is a member of many professional organizations both in the UK and Internationally. He is the author/co-author of 5 books relating to various aspects of practice and education in hypnosis, psychotherapy, and coaching.

Doodilz mindful doodling has brought our book-cover to life. A self-induced hypnotic trance inherently occurring from this relaxing, yet concentrated activity allowed Doodilz natural talent and creativity to flow through and become a powerful and magical addition to our cover design. We thank Doodilz and we are delighted that her youthful spirit has magically found its way into our book.

Jaspal Sidhu has become a convert to the power of self-hypnosis. And, she says, since editing our book, she has become smartyr too! We are deeply grateful for her invaluable contribution, expertise, and skilful editing. We are privileged that Jassy is one of our dearest friends, and we honor her as our soul sister.

Stephen Karpman A graduate of Duke University School of Medicine, Karpman was a student of Eric Berne, who founded the field of Transactional Analysis, encouraged Karpman to publish what Berne referred to as 'Karpman's Triangle' which was first described by Stephen Karpman in 1961. In psychology, The Drama Triangle is used to describe the archaic and outmoded ways in which we relate and present ourselves as victims, persecutors, and rescuers. Using an inverted triangle to map conflicted or drama-intense relationship transactions, the triangle models the power in conflicts and the destructive and shifting roles people play. It is used to describe 'roles' that we can all get caught in a hard escape cycle.

Contributors

Barbara Whitfield: As a practicing therapist in Atlanta, Georgia, she has been on the board of Directors for the Kundalini Research Network and was on the faculty of Rutgers University's Institute on Alcohol and Drug Studies for 12 years. She also spent six years researching the aftereffects of the near-death experience at the University of Connecticut Medical School. She is a consulting editor and contributor for the Journal of Near-Death Studies.

About the Authors

 **Deborah and Rizwana** are psychotherapeutic counselors and trainers who collectively bring nearly 40 years of education and experience in treating people. Their approach is grounded in evidence-based therapies, along with a psychodynamic and transcendental dimension. They utilize EMDR for trauma and hypnotherapy for mindfulness. They run their individual practices in London, UK, and work with individuals, couples, and groups. Since working together, they have co-founded the psychoeducational brand and YouTube channel Psychopedia Life.

Deborah is an integrative psychotherapeutic counselor, supervisor, and trainer. Her belief in the unlimited potential of humans drives a never-ending dedication to grow and evolve her practice. Deborah is informed by education, life experience, and spiritual practices, which allow her to bring all aspects of herself to her work, creating a unique multi-dimensional style in her approach with clients.

Rizwana is an integrative psychotherapeutic counselor and trainer. Using a unique combination of psychological and transcendental practices to support individuals, couples, and groups. Her work is rooted in treating childhood wounds and complex trauma. She works as an attachment informed EMDR therapist and hypnotherapist. Using psychoeducation as a foundation, she blends her specialties seamlessly to aid recovery and healing for a healthy and empowered life.

Printed and bound by CPI Group (UK) Ltd, Croydon, CR0 4YY